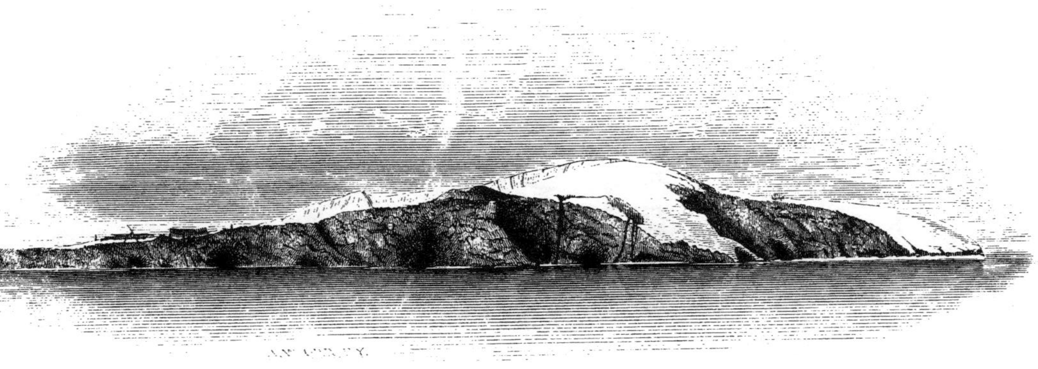

Bearing S. S. W. 2 miles. Oct. 8th. 1853.

MELBOURNE,

AND THE

CHINCHA ISLANDS;

WITH SKETCHES OF

LIMA,

AND

A VOYAGE ROUND THE WORLD.

BY
GEORGE W. PECK.

New-York:
CHARLES SCRIBNER, NASSAU-STREET,
1854.

TOBITT'S COMBINATION-TYPE,
181 *William st.*

PRINTED BY R. CRAIGHEAD,
VESEY STREET, N. Y.

CONTENTS.

PREFACE.

THERE is a peculiar propriety in my inscribing this volume to the friends through whose assistance I was enabled to undertake and complete the long voyage round the world. The book may not answer their expectation; but I hope they will believe that I shall always entertain a grateful recollection of their kindness.

Among the gentlemen to whom I was thus indebted in Melbourne, I may mention the name of His Excellency Charles Joseph Latrobe, the Lieutenant Governor of the Province of Victoria, at the time of my visit. I do so partly out of pride that as a stranger, in a city overflowing with adventurers, I should have such occasion to thank him; and partly because I am sure that the mention of his name will have the effect of introducing my sketch of Melbourne to the attention of a class of readers whom the title of the book would not otherwise attract. I shall be quite satisfied if my account of the Australian capital be found to be written in the spirit which characterizes the "Rambler in North America."

To the Honorable John Randolph Clay, the Minister of the United States in Lima, my thanks are also due for various hospitable attentions, to some of which I have elsewhere alluded.

Except the brief concluding section, and these few paragraphs, the book has been wholly written at sea, with but scanty opportunity for seclusion, and only the short intervals of freedom from interruption that a sea life affords. One necessarily goes through a great many changes of feeling under such circumstances. His own disposition varies with the state of the barometer, and he becomes sensitive to the little politics of the cabin.

I am afraid a book written in spite of such disadvantages will be found to be very unequally executed—that I may have been at times too gay, and at others too sad, too frank, or too cold. I could not avoid speaking of myself; while my natural disposition revolts from publicity, and I am too old and careworn to let myself out with the freedom which gives life to narrative. I have gone through the melancholy history of one who has had no means of life but literary labor. I have not always been able to meet its trials with resolution—never in hope. But for a few old friends, I should feel myself an outcast in the world. * * * *

Enough of this. Only let it excuse me wherein (possibly) I may have shown something of a reckless and chafed spirit in the following sketches.

Such are all the indulgences I would ask. For the rest—for the *truth* of my pictures, I can only appeal to the evidence of those who have visited the scenes described. And as to the literary merits of my work—the critics, (who may remember the corps of the Black Hussars) have now an opportunity to cut off a straggler from the camp.

New York, April 5, 1854.

PORT PHILLIP BAY.

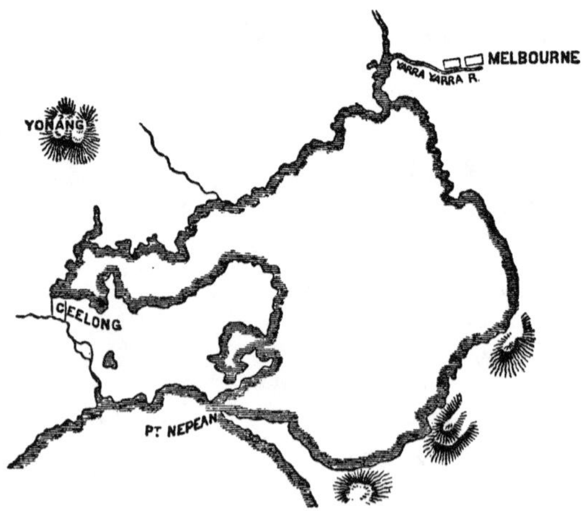

MELBOURNE, AND THE CHINCHAS.

This Tuesday, the 19th day of July, 1853, the good Ship Albus, Capt. M. B. Gregory, of Marblehead, Master, is in lat. 42° S. and lon. 154° E. from Greenwich, and is steering S. and by E. half S., under top-sails and fore-course and stay-sail, with a strong squally wind nearly abaft. In other words, she is east of the southern extremity of Van Dieman's land, and is heading for the straits which separate the two southernmost of the three islands which constitute New Zealand, through which it is intended she shall pass into the wide islandless waste of the South Pacific—a path until lately seldom traversed, except by explorers and whalemen. She is on her fourth day's sail from Port Phillip Heads, which she left last Friday, the 15th. On Saturday, as fine a day as ever was seen, she sailed through Bass's, Straits, and among its numerous beautiful rocky islets and islands, on many of which, whose names are never heard in America, there are large farms and even considerable villages. On "Deal," one of the "Kent group," we saw what seemed a comfortable country residence, standing among trees, with a lawn in front, in a valley sheltered by hills; here was a light-house nine hundred feet above the sea. The wind was light that day, and as the ship passed within two miles under the headlands, the view was quite enchanting. The square-roofed country house, just such as we may see plenty of up the Hudson, or near Boston, showing its chimneys through the strangely wild Australian pines and shrubbery, the deep green of the smooth open land, the lofty and almost perpendicular bluffs which surround the island, nowhere more than four miles across, and away in the blue sea, in a region where our home-bred fancies never stray at all, or people only with kangaroos and cannibals, altogether formed a scene to make one think how little any of us can know of the world in one short life—how vainly in the flow and change of time, we pride ourselves upon our knowledge even of what is absolute and real.

But the ship is now upon the ocean, on whose brow time writes no wrinkles, and which, though always changing, is always the same. Being in ballast only, and without cargo, she rolls deeply in the swell; the wind is getting up and the barometer falling; the grooved cabin table forms a plane of all possible inclinations, except the one parallel with the horizon; the boil of the foam is singing through the dead lights of the state rooms, and surging far astern in a broad white wake, above which the albatross are swinging; the cabin stove-pipe has "fetched away;" the steward has decided that no pig shall be slaughtered to-day; it is twelve o'clock; the Captain has retired from the deck without an observation; another *eucre* party is made up; and the author hereof sits down at the other end of the cabin table to begin this book—this wonderful book of travels and observations and sketches, beginning with MELBOURNE, the new golden city—all of which, if it is ever completed and reaches the booksellers' shelves, is to delight the "reading public" at home, some time next spring.

I flatter myself I shall be the first to have written of this new El Dorado; besides which the various incidents of long voyages are interesting. But I am not a journal-keeper. To consume paper with the little events that make up readable diaries, is one of the things I ought to have done, but have left undone. Nor am I aught of a sailor; with candid humility I must confess to having reached the antipodes in a sailing ship and not learned how to use sea terms correctly. Never mind! Sailors may smile; I shall write, and—as the Italian singer was wont to say when the audiences hissed him—"getti de moni."

My labors begin here to-day, and the grand work, if written, shall be done before I reach home, under what difficulties those mav picture to themselves who have tried a similar experiment. If I speak of "sitting down" to write, when "holding on" would have been quite as appropriate, I shall, nevertheless, write; I have promised my friends a book. There is, too, a pleasure in these pathless words—a companionship in the art of recalling and narrating. It helps to preserve one's identity. It keeps me in mind that I am not Captain Cook, or Sir Joseph Banks, or Lieutenant Wilkes, but only a wandering "member of the press."

WEDNESDAY, 20th.—After a late dinner yesterday, the eating of which required sufficient gymnastic exercise to insure its digestion, the wind continued rising and at the same time hauling southward, until in the evening it blew a strong gale, with heavy squalls from the S. S. W. The ship being so light, lay over and rolled fearfully, though more easily than might have been expected. At nine o'clock we were under close reefed main top-sail and fore-sail, the fore top-sail having been split in a squall an hour before. We passengers began to think of the probabilities of the ship's "shifting ballast," "broaching to," and the like, not without some reason; for she is so light that lying-to in such a wind must take her down almost to her beam ends, and if she were to scud before it for twenty-four hours, we dreaded being jammed on the coast of New Zealand two hundred miles distant. We "turned in" (literally, for there was no such thing as getting in any other way) early, and I fell asleep, wishing myself in Boston jail; and strange to say, was dreaming pleasantly of things that happened long ago, when a more sudden lurch than usual nearly pitched me out of my bunk about two o'clock in the morning. I went on deck; the moon was shining, the cloud squalls driving over in grand masses, the sea running mountains, the wind not a wind, but a fierce pitiless Power, triumphing in loud victory—in screaming excess and rage—over the treacherous deep, the ship a mere bit of driftwood, no one visible on deck but the second mate and the two men at the wheel, the rigging howling, or rather shrieking that sharp prolonged shriek which when seamen hear, they say "the drummer and fifer have come on board!" (burlesquing what is too horrible for direct comparison;) add the consciousness of being in a remote ocean, the nearest coast the least known of the southern large islands of New Zealand, inhabited doubtless by tattooed Maoris, with more taste for the white man's body than his literature; also the other consciousness of being perfectly helpless, and with no better claim on the indulgence of Providence than the thousands who have found rest beneath stormy seas; add, also,—but I was too cold and sleepy to have a "realizing sense" of anything, and so after a brief space I "turned in" again. In the phrase of Lord Bacon somewhere quoted, I rather "noted" than "liked" it. Before morning we had some fierce hail squalls, after one of which the hail lay three inches deep on the lee side of the deck; but I heard nothing till breakfast time. At that hour the cabin group would have presented a study for an artist. At 2 P. M., the wind still continues a gale, and the sea is tremendous, though the squalls are not so violent as they were during the night. Our position to-day by observation is in lat. 44° 14' south, and lon. 161° east from Greenwich.

FRIDAY, 22d.—The gale was so severe yesterday that I did not feel in the humor of writing. The squalls grew more frequent and heavy, the glass refused to rise, the sky looked thicker, more sails were split, Kangaroo, the half-native dog took to howling, plates got smashed, the cook "blasphemed," (so the second steward informed us,) and there was a general "turn in" after an attempt at an early dinner. For myself, though blessed with as good a constitution that way as most, I cannot sleep twenty-four hours out of twelve to conform to any state of the weather; so I rolled in my berth two hours by the ship's bell, though they seemed to me two eternities, and mentally reviewed my "past history," and "present condition," and "future prospects." I thought of

——"bliss forever lost,
Of fair occasions, gone forever by
Of hopes too fondly nursed, too rudely crossed;
Of many a cause to wish—yet fear to die."

Though I neither court or avoid, and least of all would

discourage such a habit of thinking, yet it comes to me often enough in the natural way; and sometimes I fancy I get more than my share of it. Accordingly I now endeavored to create a diversion by sketching out various plans to be pursued in the production of this remarkable work. But none of them suited. I am convinced that this rolling and pitching and quivering, even when it does not cause sea-sickness, weakens the power of the mind. I feel my brain oscillate up and down against the *pia mater*, and am occupied with so many varieties of the sensation, that there is no concentration or logical sequence of ideas. I turn on the will, as many atmospheres to the inch as the cranium can bear; still there is no regular action. A few revolutions, and the engine stops, reverses, starts too fast or too slow, and produces no available result. After many such trials I have resolved to write on, in a mighty maze, entirely without a plan, just as the Miltons and Shakspeares of our day write verses. This frame of mind comes all the more irresistibly upon me from my having left Melbourne so recently, where I am sure no man can preserve his sanity long without careful effort.

Thus I lay musing and half-dozing, until a sudden row on deck, followed by a decided change in the angle of my berth, disturbed me, and I climbed *out of* what I had pitched *into*, and, emerging, found written on the slate on the cabin table the following :—

"3 *P. M.* Lat. 44° 58′ S., Lon. 162° 53′ E. Bore up for the North Cape. Finding it very rough, and our sails giving out, think it prudent to go to the Northward."

So we are not to attempt the South Pacific at this season (mid-winter !) How very sorry I am ! Perhaps we may be obliged to stop at some one of the islands for water or vegetables. Very well. It is the first time this long while I have felt a thrill of romance. I feel it to-day ; the wind blows fresh, and we are swaying along with top-gallants set, and yards braced sharp up, direct for the North extremity of New Zealand—thence for the great Pacific archipelago and the calmer seas and more genial breezes of the tropics.

Saturday, 23d.—The wind continues fresh with occasional squalls. It has hauled a little more aft this morning, and we are ploughing through the surges finely, with just such a motion as a horse would have at a canter, if horses were as large as ships. The sky is magnificent with piled up clouds, and the strong breeze crests the deep blue waves as far as eye can see. We are now nearly abreast of the northernmost of the New Zealand islands; two days more, if the wind holds, will fetch us round the North Cape.

It is impossible not to feel exhilarated. I fancy sailors acquire something of their gallant and reckless disposition from unconsciously feeling that they control, and thus identifying themselves with the motions of the ship. It is certainly the proudest and grandest motion that can be attained, and so lifelike that the vessel *is* a living creature. I leaned over the head a long while this morning, watching the foam and the heaving waves, and the far-off horizon; and dreaming of the beauty of the world and the strangeness of life. Such moments, when we lose ourselves in nature, are the sleep of the reflective faculty, and they infuse new vigor into the soul. No art can convey what we experience in them; it is the efflorescence of the spirit; the fruit must ripen afterwards. When I think of attempting to repaint such oceanic panoramas I smile at myself, a sickly smile, and my heart grows small. I am constitutionally too fond of speculation.

WEDNESDAY, 27th.—As I foretold, we doubled the North Cape of New Zealand, day before yesterday. About forty miles from the Cape itself there is a group of islets called "The Three Kings," in sight of which we passed at nightfall. Yesterday we were becalmed all day; but I could neither write or play the violin in the cabin while the men were holystoning the poop deck. In the afternoon we had a passing call from a school of black-fish, whose mottled backs made them seem like a herd of cows grazing in a meadow. To day the wind is still light; the ocean wide and blue. I have no perpetual sense of its boundlessness. As I look back upon my voyagings, it is as when I have travelled inland. Sometimes I have gone through deep woods; these are the storms. Then we have passed over high rolling uplands; in clear strong breezes—through a broken rocky country in squalls; and on such days as this across broad plains. The sense of infinite expansion is greater in looking off upon the ocean from a promontory, or in casual glimpses from the turnings of a country road.

Another odd effect is, that while I feel the poetry of the ocean, and the health-breathing spirit of it, my mind perversely recoils from it. I have a craving for everything that is in opposition to it; for metaphysics, for example, or æsthetical reveries upon music, and the like. I am a living witness to the truth of the saying that "*cœlum non animum mutant, qui trans mare currunt.*" Let no one take a long voyage to *forget*—to court oblivion. The Lethe does not flow into the ocean; I doubt if there be any such river at all. But out of all this wondering at finding oneself under a new heaven, and the excitement, and dread, and expectation, and general upheaval of the elements within, there may come "strength for what remains." Last night the moon ascended over long, soft outlined ranks of clouds, and the Southern Cross stood clear in the mid heavens—emblem of patience, and hope, and mercy.

Travellers have great facilities for making themselves acquainted with remote countries. Here is a view of New

Zealand taken on the spot by one who nearly circumnavigated that group. Its accuracy will be vouched for by all my fellow passengers. It will be perceived from it that the land is generally high and apparently barren, if not rocky.

THE THREE KINGS,
BEARING S. E. 14 MILES.

SUNDAY, 31st.—For the last three days we have lain-to in a severe gale from the south-east—dead ahead. I think I may boast hereafter that I have heard the wind blow. It has not wholly abated to-day, but the sun has come out—we are moving ahead a little with a reef shaken out of the main top-sail and course, and newly-repaired fore-top-sail and fore-sail all braced aft; the ship has just pitched out of the inkstand I hold in my hand a blot upon the page which the Printer cannot imitate; altogether affairs are, as the Melbourne phrase is, more "serene."

SUNDAY, 31st.—"When two Sundays come together" is not after all an impossible condition. To-day we pass the 180th degree of longitude east from Greenwich in lat. 33° south, and now begin to reckon longitude WEST. Here we fuse two days into one to correct for the twelve hours we have gained since passing the Greenwich meridian. But since New York is in 73° west, I have come 253 degrees, and am sixteen hours and forty minutes ahead of Trinity clock—to say nothing of having spent nearly two winters in the year. The distance home seems quite short. It is only 107° of longitude, and from 33° south to 41° north—in fact, the distance is nothing, as Mr. Micawber observed, "comparatively speaking."

WEDNESDAY, 10th.—After a week of fair weather, and leading winds generally light, we had another heavy blow come on yesterday afternoon, which lasted during the night. I think the gale was for a few hours yet more severe than any we have experienced. Sleep was out of the question. At noon to-day it had died away to a light breeze and now we are knocking about in almost a dead calm, under a thick misty rain—everybody in excellent humor, of course, after the night, and with this delightful motion. At dinner we stuck to the cabin floor, like so many flies on the wall of a room. The second steward, last night, coming down the cabin stairs, allowed the perpendicular drawn through his centre of gravity to fall without the base, in consequence of which seven out ot ten coffee cups went " to smash."

We are in about 40° south and 141° west—nearly half way across the great Pacific, whose beautiful islands lie leagues away to the northward. I have had hopes of our stopping at Easter Island; but unless we have winds not likely to blow here, I must resign them and content myself with our very satisfactory survey of the coast of New Zealand.

Let me here record that one day last week, I caught a cape pigeon and have stuffed his skin for preservation—with what success remains to be seen.

FRIDAY, 12th.—This morning we have been rolling along with a strong breeze under courses and double reefed top-sails. At breakfast the sun was out bright, and the ocean wide awake, dancing under us in dark blue mountains, flinging spray from their snowy summits all along the misty horizon.

A little before ten, we made a sail about a point on the weather bow; the first we have seen. She kept off, and we passed several miles to windward of her after dinner. We are to day in lon. 135°, lat. 36° nearly. Since dinner the wind has risen and we have had some very heavy squalls with rain. The crew are now close reefing the main top-sail, the fore top-sail having been split, and the courses furled before. In half an hour or less, we shall be lying-to, most probably in a gale and a very heavy sea; a state of things it may be pleasant to read of—in case we survive it and the others that may succeed it. Otherwise, geologists estimate the average depth of the ocean to be about five miles.

MONDAY, 15th.—We are to-day in lon. 120° lat. 39° south, a fine breeze, as much as we want, well aft. In the last seven days we have come nearly fifteen hundred miles; and if the wind holds as it is a few days more, we shall probably make Callao in a fortnight. But farewell to the Cannibal islands! I have come down to the great waters but have seen very little of their wonders—not even a whale, except a thin spirt just visible one day afar off, which they say was a spout.

WEDNESDAY, 24th.—For nearly a week the wind has been dead a-head, and we have run southward of our course. Yesterday we were in lon. 120° nearly, and still down in lat. 37°. To-day it is cloudy and almost calm, and we are creeping slowly over a gray, hazy ocean. A sail is reported from aloft, far away on the starboard bow; but I have not been able to makeout anything from the mizen-top.

FRIDAY, 26th.—The same wind and much the same weather. Yesterday morning a sail, supposed, from her course and the boats on her quarter, to be a homeward-bound whaler, crossed our bows and went out of sight on the lee quarter. About noon another came in sight to windward, which finally luffed up within far speaking distance, and passed under our stern. She proved to be the bark Laurens of New York, bound, as well as could be understood, to Baltimore. She appeared full, and was probably from Callao.

SUNDAY, 28th.—A fair wind at last. The ship is rolling and pitching along over a heavy broken swell, at the rate of seven or eight knots an hour, with her nose direct for her port of destination—only eighteen hundred miles distant. We have now splendid sky views; the clouds have the softened straw-colored tints peculiar to the great ocean, and the sun-rises and sun-sets are almost unnaturally splendid. Sometimes long lines stretch away to a horizon almost boundless. At others, the piles of vapor reach up immeasurably overhead, so that the whole heavens appear enlarged. The moon is almost at her change, and the Southern Cross passes its meridian early in the evening over our starboard quarter.

TUESDAY, SEPT. 6th.—The fair wind lasted but a few hours. Days and weeks pass on and bring nothing but calms and light contrary winds. We are now about eleven hundred miles from port, in lat. 78° south, and lon. 87°

west, the nearest land being the island of St. Felix, two hundred miles westward. The sun has scarcely shown himself these four days. Several sails have been seen far away; one is in sight this morning far to windward. Two fin back whales gave us a passing look—one of them I saw; he was quite near and must have been a large one; sixty feet long, we judged. Most of the time the ocean is just deepened in hue by a light ripple, and we scarcely feel its sleepy breathing motion. Drowsy, dyspeptic, discontented.

Thursday, 8th.—Last evening came the long wished-for fair wind, and to-day we are running with studding-sails set, right before it. There is only a long gentle swell, and the breeze is steady like the trades, which we should suppose it was if it came from a few points east instead of west or south. We now average a fin-back in the distance daily, and the schools of porpoises are frequent enough to prove that this part of the ocean ought to be well educated.

Sept. 14th.—Anchored in Callao Roads.

I.

MELBOURNE.

Melbourne is situated on the north side of and two miles inland from the head of a nearly land-locked circular bay, about forty miles across. On the left of this bay, about midway, is the harbor and town of Geelong—a young city, numbering already nearly thirty thousand inhabitants, and beautifully situated in a fine agricultural district. The bay is sometimes called "the Bay," and oftener "Port Phillip," which was originally the name of the Colony, and is not now the name of any particular place; perhaps it will be most convenient to style it "Port Phillip Bay."

The ship Plymouth Rock, in which I sailed from Boston on the 18th of February, anchored in the immediate harbor or roadstead of Melbourne, (Hobson's Bay,) on the afternoon of the 20th of May. We had made Cape Otway, the first land we saw of the coast of New Zealand, early on the morning of Monday, the 16th. This Cape, on which there is a light-house, is at the entrance of Bass' Straits, and is about ninety miles southwesterly from the entrance to Port Phillip Bay; that day we made about half the distance, and stood off and on under a light wind during the night. In the morning there was a heavy fog and almost a dead calm; the wind continued very light the whole day, and when we reached Point Nepean, at the entrance of Port Phillip, about four in the afternoon, there was just air enough stirring to keep steerage way on the vessel, while the strong tide took her through the narrow channel—not more than a mile wide for ships. It was a fine afternoon, and the apparently grassy field around the lighthouse on the bluff two miles to the left, with the half dozen or more vessels at anchor in the bay, had quite a home look after a long voyage. Presently, in answer to the signal, a pilot came on board, who instantly became an object of as much curiosity to our seventy or eighty down east gold-seekers, as if he had been a veritable *ornithorhyncus paradoxus*, instead of a live Englishman, with a face deeply scarred by the small-pox. The contrast of his voice with the nasal tones of " down east," was quite remarkable.

At night-fall it became calm again, and we came to anchor under the high land, called Arthur's Seat, in the east channel. The calm continued all next day with a heavy fog; we had the anchor up but did not make ten miles. About midnight a little breeze rippled the still water, and we got under weigh, and proceeded slowly up the bay, till, as the day advanced, we came to anchor, as aforesaid, in the afternoon. On the left, going up, the land is low and flat, except some distant and isolated highlands; on the right it is higher, but the curves of the hills are gentle, and the view presents nothing striking

It was near sun-set when our last sails were furled, and we lay near the lighthouse at Williamstown—one among a fleet of more than three hundred mostly first class vessels, that lay around us in the bay, or rather the mouth of the Yarra-Yarra River, called a bay. On the right of this bay, is the tent-built village of Sandridge, and two miles beyond it in a direct line, Melbourne, the smoke, and the two principal church towers of which we could see. Melbourne is on the north bank of the Yarra-Yarra, which, after leaving it, makes a complete bend, or "oxbow," of ten miles or more, flowing westward in passing the town, and eastward at its mouth. Williamtown, at the mouth of the river on a point directly across from Sandridge, is on the south, though on the same side with Melbourne; little steamers run to and fro from here to the city round the bend, almost every hour of the day.

After we had anchored, the Customs and Health Officers visited us, and we were then told to make ready for going ashore early in the morning. Accordingly next morning found us piled on one of the miniature tug steamers that ply about the bay; boxes, chests, trunks of all imaginable shapes, mattrasses, bundles of spades, and other utensils for gold-digging, and passengers, all so jammed up, we had just room to stand. We passed, I remember, a ship recently arrived laden with one of Mrs. Caroline Chisholm's invoices of young women for the Colony. Several of the fascinating creatures appeared leaning over the bulwarks, and waved their handkerchiefs in answer to the cheers of Jonathans, trebly gallant after a three months voyage. One of the papers afterwards, I observed, in speaking of this fair ship load, characterised it as a "well selected lot." And truly some of them whom I saw in the streets, did appear well fitted to become the wives of shepherds, and tamers of wild men and wild continents—tall, strong English girls, six feet high, with simple healthy faces, and immense ankles, stepping three yards at a step. Several of them would have made a sensation in the streets of Boston, where the health and complexion of young women are less regarded than their "intellectuality." I could not but fancy these rosy colonists thronging to hear infidel sermons and coming home to argue thereupon over cold baked beans! And how would the lady of my affections, the landlady of the "Hedgers," who gave us rump-steak pie enough for three at a meal, uplift her hands in pitying horror, could she behold upon what meats, or rather what deprivation of meats, the over-conscientious New England mothers in our villages, nurse their broods of consumptive undervoters!

I shall not attempt to describe the dirt, noise, and "hideous combustion" in which we were emptied upon the wharf. Some of my readers may remember years ago fighting for their valises with Albany hackmen; it was nothing to this. Only here the difficulty was to know what to have done, and how to find any one to do it. I questioned a decent looking stranger, and followed his advice. It being impossible to have my luggage taken to any public house, I had it stored near the wharf at a shilling a week per parcel, in a thin shingled house, along with about five hundred cords of other trunks, bedding and the like. It cost eight shillings (two dollars) more for cartage, and the things might as well have remained at home for all the good they did me after they were stored. In respect of linen, and all that, I was in advance of the age, even in Melbourne—which is saying something.

II.

I PRESUME all Americans who visited Melbourne last summer, must have been struck with the first view of the town, looking east from the market place across the valley through Collins street. This is, or was, the Broadway of the place; it is very wide—much wider than our Broadway—and as it curves down the valley and rises on the other side, just as Broadway does from Leonard to Canal and thence to Houston street, only that the curve is shorter and deeper, the whole of the busiest part of it is visible at once. There are many city-like buildings upon it, and it is lined mostly with retail shops. As I walked down towards the Argus office, which is on the rise at the other end, I could almost fancy myself in New York. Perhaps this impression was aided by my seeing many faces whilom not unknown in ——— street, and elsewhere. And here let me observe, that I never had any particular horror of the sporting gentry on account of their profession. I have known many good fellows in that walk of life—men whom I would trust as soon as others, except in the way of cards. That I myself never gamed may be owing more to circumstances than to any power of resisting the temptation to do so. And besides, it is almost impossible to succeed in the world as a gamester without imbibing a taste for the fine arts, and a habit of counterfeiting the manners and conversation of gentlemen. On the whole, therefore, I think the society of enterprising gamblers, those who do business on an extensive scale, I mean, and take an honest pride in their calling, far preferable to that of many who are engaged in less hazardous speculations.

My face was probably as well known to several gentlemen of this class whom I saw in my first walk, as theirs to me. I could scarcely help smiling occasionally, a sort of half smile of recognition, as much as if I had said in the memorable words of Grimaldi, "Little boys! I see you!" —particularly when my eyes lighted upon Eben, of Boston, learned in the law, whose footsteps no more gladden the corridors of Tudor's Building.

Collins-street runs parallel with the Yarra-Yarra river, and is built upon for nearly two miles, reckoning from beyond King-street west, to the other extremity east, towards Richmond. It is the third street from the river. The first is Flinders-street, if street it can be called, which is generally a slough. Then comes Flinders Lane, where at the time of my leaving, it was reported that soundings had been obtained through the mud, at thirty fathoms. This, however, was thought to be an under estimate for the average depth. Then succeeds Collins-street, Little Collins street; Burke and Little Burke; Lonsdale, and Little Lonsdale; Latrobe—and so on. The little streets are narrow, the others very broad. These are intercepted by streets rising north and south, making rectangular squares or "blocks," like those in the upper part of New-York; thus from the east are King-street, William, Queen, Elizabeth, Swanston, Russell, Stevens, and I know not how many more. These are built upon at an average distance of more than a mile from the river, and some of them, Elizabeth and Swanston, for example, are the finest in the city.

Even the space included in the above would form a large town, but over-stocked as it is, and bursting out into innumerable avenues of tents and shanties, it does not contain more than half of the population. Over the height of land to the north-east is Collingwood, already an immense suburb; and I wish I could show the reader, as in a panorama, how the tide of human life is flowing over the wide green plains beyond—green at mid-winter, and over-shadowed at the base of the distant hills by the evergreen foliage of the park like gum-tree forests. Eastward, through the spacious and beautiful St. James' Park, along the banks of the

Yarra-Yarra, is Richmond, another arm of the city; and beyond it St. Kilda and Brighton, on the bay. Across the Yarra-Yarra, over the splendid bridge, the most imposing public work the city boasts, built of stone, with a single arch, of one hundred and fifty feet span, is Canvastown, a city of tents, Emerald Hill, and Sandridge—the latter of which it is no exaggeration to say, doubles its population as often as once a quarter.

When it is remembered that every building, hut and tent was crowded with tenants, it may be imagined how animated the principal streets of the business part of Melbourne appeared to a "new chum" just from a long lonely voyage. Collins-street, as I passed down it the first morning, was as thronged as Broadway. I stopped on the Elizabeth street corner, and took an observation. Long teams of as many as twenty yoke of bullocks to each, were drawing single wagons up and down—giving one a not too favorable impression with regard to the state of the roads out of the town. Rough horses, the roughest and shabbiest that can be conceived, were cantering to and fro, ridden by men with long boots, stuck far into short stirrups, and who seemed to urge their forlorn beasts along by jumping in their saddles, and elevating their elbows. Heavy chaise carts, and dog carts, horse killing vehicles, unknown in the United States—ponies with errand-boys, and dray-carts with veteran hacks, in the last stages of decline, filled up the middle of the street. Upon the side-walk was a mot ley throng, all with busy faces and "speculation" in their eyes—a few clean and well-dressed, in the English fashion, Melbourne exquisites—the major part a mixture of jockey and farmer, with long boots or gaiters, and loaded whips; merchants with eager calculating eyes, Jews of all nations and combinations; swells of low degree, Parsees and Chinese, sportsmen, convicts, or those on whose tell-tale countenances, "jail-bird," was plainly written (of those there was no lack)—a few well dressed ladies, in long skirts draggled with mud, servant girls and such, policemen in blue uniform, escorts in ditto, with white facing, now and then a soldier—and so on, down to the unshorn, unwashed, almost undressed rabble, whether composed of disappointed diggers, or what, I know not—but exhibiting some of the lowest and dirtiest specimens I ever saw in my life. There was, at least, so I fancied, a head-strong reckless energy of movement in everything. I seemed to feel as if a great stream of life were dashing by in a torrent—loud, violent, impetuous, uncontrollable. It was impossible not to be susceptible to the sympathetic influences of the scene. Though I had no hope of making money, and consequently nothing directly in common with the throng of wealth seekers, and was indeed occupied by much more vexing cares, I could not help feeling a sort of factitious vitality. "*Sessa!*" methought, "Let the world slide. This week is at least mine, and I will revel in observation."

III.

I THINK I under-estimate the population of Melbourne and its suburbs, during the month I was there, as an average of one hundred thousand souls. Of course there were thousands daily passing upward to the mines; but there were thousands also returning, and every ship-load that arrived left its residuum in the city. All its immediate neighborhoods were encampments. The whole vicinity was overspreading with the devastation of human presence, like an oasis in the desert on which a locust swarm has lighted. The simile is not a forced one; for wherever the crowd of settlers had reached, there was mud and filthy crawling creatures in old clothes, defacing the natural green of the primeval open land. I could not but moralize the spectacle; wherever I looked, the earth seemed so fair, and man and his labors so vermin-like, that I felt vile. Is man indeed the "paragon of animals," or only a parasitic insect, a disease of the earth's cuticle, analagous to those species, with whose fair proportions the solar microscope so appals the shuddering sense?

The Yarra-Yarra is a narrow, muddy, winding stream, which comes from somewhere eastward, and with its adjacent bottoms, occupies a large space in the map of Melbourne; partly on account of its being dammed below the bridge, about midway of the front street, in order to afford the town a supply of fresh water. The name Yarra-Yarra, is said to be in the native language, "flowing, flowing;" and the river is so named, because it does not dry up in the summer, like most Australian streams. It is navigable for vessels drawing ten feet of water up to the dam, though for much of the way it is hardly more than sufficiently wide for two vessels to pass abreast. The tide rises to the foot of the dam, over which there is a fall of about four feet, designed to keep the fresh water of the river (which is as much discolored as that of the Ohio in its high stages,) from the salt water of the bay. But I observed that the water is pumped out, to be carted about the town for five shillings per load, at the foot of Elizabeth-street, a little above the dam. The whole sewerage of the river slopes of the broad streets of the upper part of the city, therefore, flows towards the Yarra-Yarra, though it may be partly diverted by a cross sewer; and I heard of extensive sheep washing establishments further up, towards Richmond. At all events, just above the bridge, there were always grooms riding in horses to wash; and the gutters of Swanston and Elizabeth streets, flowing towards the river, were not by any means the cleanest gutters in the world; it was rare to walk that way of a morning without seeing several dogs in them, in various stages of decomposition, and generally as many more, just alive, suffering from a singular distemper, then prevalent in the town, as mortal to dogs as the plague to men. Often, when disposed to quaff a draught of the "flowing, flowing," have I "mentally ejaculated," as Laura Matilda would write, "Heaven preserve my stomach from the braes of Yarra!"

But I know not why I should be so severe upon the poor river, which doubtless does its best to keep itself clean, when the whole town ought to be characterized as the paradise of the Dirty Club. Much of its want of cleanliness must be set down to the account of its situation in a region of mud and dirt,—the crowd that overwhelms it, and the eagerness of its people to reap the golden harvest every moment as it ripens. But Jonathan is certainly neater than his elder brother—not in his person maybe, but in his "fixings," his appointments. He contrives to have everything more comfortable about him. He may not build so substantially; he may talk through his nose, and chew tobacco out of doors, but at home he is under a government that obliges him to be rather particular. One may see the difference on going from the States into any English colony, or in any of our large manufacturing towns where there are operatives enough from Birmingham or Manchester to occupy a quarter by themselves. English tourists have often noticed the neatness of the dwellings in our cities. Perhaps it is owing to differences in climate and constitution; our continent has not the insular fog; we are not so universally accustomed to the use of bituminous coal; we are more excitable and sensitive; less thick-skinned. However it may be, the general fact is indisputable.

I do not think a Yankee population could by any force of circumstances, short of actual *vis major*, ever sink to the Melbourne zero of discomfort. If they did, they could not long survive it. In all the new towns of the west, and in California, wherever they have migrated, they bring in their wake clean food and beds undefiled. True, I was but a month in Melbourne, and that in the best season; I did not experience one of the dry hot winds they speak of which blow in summer from the great unexplored deserts when the dust gathers like snow inches deep through the chinks of closed doors and windows; I saw enough to excuse much, however, in the mud. Still, justice must be done; and in point of cleanliness, Melbourne, by her own confession, must be found wanting. She has acquired colonial habits, and unless she speedily reforms, she must suffer for them in the health of her citizens. I am sad when I think of the probable consequences of the present or past state of things continuing through many sultry seasons.

The history of my first few days in Melbourne will show what all who visited it had to encounter on arriving. My first *essai* was for the Argus office, to the editor of which journal, the only one heard of in America, I intended to offer a full file of the New York and Boston papers of the date of my departure. The office is, comparatively speaking, a somewhat imposing range of cement-covered houses on the right hand of Collins street, and beyond the valley to the East. It was not without considerable difficulty that I was able to find a gentleman in the editorial department to whom I could offer my intended courtesy—which was, however, at length well enough received, though quite differently to what it would have been by any of our offices at home. I may mention in passing, that all the use the Argus ever made of the papers, was the insertion three days after of a paragraph of ship news, relative to the sailing of the Bavaria from New York for Port Phillip; and it was nearly a week before I could obtain them again, when they had ceased to be of any use to me, though I had expressly requested that they might be returned after the news had been "cut" from them. But of the Melbourne journals hereafter.

By dinner time I was quite tired. But having no place in which to sit down, except the bar rooms, I wandered on until one of my fellow-passengers met and conducted me to Passmore's Commercial Hotel, where many more of them were to dine in the saloon afterwards used for the Fourth of July dinner.

In the afternoon we found a room where we could all sit together; but this was quite as fatiguing to me as walking. So I wandered forth again, to inquire for some reasonably quiet accommodations, for Passmore's could only afford a "stretcher" for the night. I met at the Shakespeare some young Boston merchants, and after tea—in the shape of a cold mutton pie at a baker's shop—followed them and two or three gentlemen who had come with me in the Plymouth Rock, to the Metropolitan, the American hotel *par excellence* of Melbourne, and which could boast a civil bar-keeper, who was at least a graduate of Tammany Hall. Here we spent an hour or so congratulating ourselves and being congratulated on our safe arrival, though I was so fatigued I could scarcely keep my eyes open. I should have said that through the noise and excitement I had slept only in snatches since we entered the Bay, and in fact for several nights previous—our youthful gold-hunters having, in the overflow of their joy at seeing the land where most of them will probably leave their bones, indulged in midnight charivaris till they were stopped by "request" of Captain Caldwell.

At the hotel we kept it up as well as we could till near eleven, and then were shown in a body to our sleeping apartment—the concert or dancing hall of the house. Here we bestowed ourselves, forty or fifty of us, as it happened, some on settees, some on the table, some on "stretchers," or frail narrow cots, and others on the floor. I thought myself "cute" in appropriating and defending my claim to a stretcher. Alas, it was a foot too short! and worst of all, I had hardly got into a sound sleep after the general row, sleepy wit, groans, wise remarks, and all that, had subsided, when down came the head of my "stretcher," and I was obliged to tack ship to avoid congestion of the brain. I did not seem to have slept at all, when I woke a little after daylight, and started with a few others to go over to Canvasstown and visit our mining friends who had encamped there. I think I was never so completely fagged out in my life. The morning was fine, but I could just drag my limbs to the nearest tent, and throw myself upon some bedding, when I slept almost at once, a heavy leaden sleep, from which I woke some time in the forenoon, a little less fatigued, but unrefreshed. I adjourned to a large tent on which was painted "EUROPEAN BOARDING AND LODGING HOUSE." It was divided into two compartments, one for eating, the other for sleeping. I got some "tea," (Gunpowder, by the taste,) and among some old books in a corner found, strange to say, the remnant of a Virgil, with which and the "tea," (horresco referens! but it was at least hot,) I amused myself until dinner time—the first two hours of actual repose I had experienced since leaving the ship. After it I gained courage to go over to the city —intending to return to lodge at night. Perhaps it was well I did not, for the next neighbor on the contiguous row of beds to one of my fellow-passengers died during the night; and when the "insatiate archer" was aiming so near, he might, like Billy Kirby, not have "allowed for the wind," in which case this invaluable work would never have been written.

As it grew towards evening I began to argue with myself whether it were better to suffer the ills I had, or fly to others which I knew not of. It was come to that pass that I had but one desire left—to sleep. The European Boarding and Lodging House did not promise much. I looked in at the Royal Hotel, which appeared to be the leading mercantile house—fell in with an American citizen, a man of the world, whom I fancy to myself smiling as he reads this, and on his recommendation I engaged a lodging there, and awaited the hour of retiring full of cheerful anticipation. Alas! how seldom does the event realize our fondest anticipations of future bliss!

They gave me a bed in number thirteen—an ominous number. There were three in the room—narrow, iron, with bars a foot apart running athwart-ships, occupied by three sufferers, two besides myself. It was cold; the covering was insufficient; the whole arrangement too short. Hark! what was that?—A musquito? It is—a chilly musquito, too cold to hum and dying of hunger. And there is another—and another—and another—no end to them! I wrap my face in the soiled sheet and doze. Ha! what is this? Can it be possible that there are *fleas* too? It is—not only possible, but undeniable. In thousands—myriads. Farewell sleep—the innocent sleep. I thought of Job, and Regulus, and the Chinese torture. I got out and shook the sheets; laid my body out and swathed it in them. In vain! I tried the floor: I was pursued. The bed again; and so tossed and groaned out the night—a night longer than the winter nights at Spitzbergen. A single flea will wake me at any time; I had rather be stung by a wasp; but now their name was legion, and I dare say I afforded them an agreeable change of diet. I shall never forget in what agony I looked for daylight through the flat window in the roof, (the room was an attic;) how I hailed the first faint gloaming, and spun out the thread of my patience till I could distinguish far below, the cheerful bar bell. Then I rose and cooled my swollen eyelids with a spoonful of Yarra, combed my locks with my fingers, donned coat and hat, descended, and with a desperation of manner and voice that admitted of no denial, ordered Mr. Jones to furnish instantly for my refreshment a "spider!"

Such was my introduction to Melbourne. In the afternoon, beginning to fancy I could not survive much longer without rest, I went to an apothecary and prescribed for myself nine Dover's powders, such as they still cross babies witn, had them put up in three pills, got myself through special favor put up into a single-bedded room, took my pills, rolled myself up in my boots, and—slept—a long, refreshing sleep, from which I woke late next day, a new man. After this I retained the same room all the while I was in Melbourne. It was bad enough—an attic, half-furnished with a narrow camp bedstead, rickety chair and table, cold and never clean, though Jane the convict girl, a good-natured creature, beloved of John, used to wash it daily, so that it was seldom dry. The mosquitos vanished as we approached the midwinter month of July, and the fleas either gradually retired, or which amounted to the same thing, the surface deposit accumulated on their victim, where washing is impossible, to such an extent that they annoyed him no more. I had no luxury of repose, it is true; the month was altogether a most uncomfortable one, as will appear incidentally; but, like the camomile, which, the more it is trodden on the faster it grows—so the human plant sometimes thrives best in discomfort and anxiety.

IV.

Rough, loud, and unquiet as thou wert, O city of the Antipodes, ungently and inhospitably as thou receivedst strangers—thou Melbourne, from whose bourne few travellers return—I yet remember thee as a cheering dream. I saw with regret the green plains around thee, and the distant hills grow blue and low on the far horizon. Even as I write, my thoughts go back to thee not as to a locality from which I have escaped, but as to a city where, if I could have forgotten the affections and duties that seem to call me homeward—if I could have let the good-bye that I bade my mother been the last in life, or if I could have been content to feed my soul forever with the image of that ideal lady, my heart's mistress, whose realization I

3

am sure I shall never behold out of my native land, and probably never there—I could have projected myself into a life of enterprise, and lived out my hour as unforebodingly as the rest of thy busy multitude.

The site of Melbourne is beautiful. That is hardly the word either. It is magnificent. The lines of the landscapes around it are in long undulations open to the sky. The heart of the town is a broad valley extending out northwardly to more elevated plains. The higher portions east and west overlook this valley, and around in the distance the view is bounded by the sea line of the Bay, and the wavy outline of mountain ranges forty and fifty miles away. The landscape seems everywhere to be laid out upon a large scale; the views westward from the Telegraph Hill, or eastward from beyond St. James's Church, looking over Collingwood, are especially grand and unique —full of the character we image at home as belonging to this vast remote region. They are antipodial, primeval—glimpses of mighty solitudes, the ends of the earth. Whether their effect might not have been attributable to my own preconception or to the natural surprise I could never shake off in the effort to reassure myself that I was where I was, is of no consequence. Had they not harmonized with such feelings, I could not have been so affected by them.

I think the view westward from the Government House particularly fine though the elements of it are the simplest possible. On the left the bay and forest of shipping; on the right the sloping curves of the Mount Macedon range, fifty miles off, and intervening rolling forest plains; directly in front, a dead level extending from the base of the uplands of the city across immense green watery meadows, more than half lake, but not marshy, for they are dotted with herds of cattle—to green plains where the eye can distinguish here and there a shepherd's station; thence onward over I know not how many miles of perfect flat to an outline broken only by the Youang Mountains, which rise from it like islands from the horizon of the ocean. To my apprehension there is a decided character of lordliness in the outlines of these hills; they repose on the plain with the air of a giant resting on his elbow, and gazing unconcernedly over the illimitable waste of the Southern Pacific. I could never look towards them, as they are seen from the east and west streets of Melbourne, without experiencing an awakening sensation; I could not bring myself to fancy them inanimate. At the hazard of the seer and sketcher's reputation, behold them retraced from memory.

THE YOUANG MOUNTAINS.

The plains, it must be remembered, are as unbroken as here represented ; but no sketch can give the effect of the distance, the immense green level, and the airy blue of the mountains.

Round the northward the mountains are higher, but less characteristic ; the principal are the Macedon range, and farther inland, the Dandonong, and for aught I could ascertain, the gold-encircled summits of the Korong—glorious names for the old monarchs of these ancient wildernesses.

Beyond Collingwood north-east, the view extends over a grassy plain of several miles in width, over which the tide of human population is spreading like the debris of a mountain torrent, to the base of similar nameless highlands —or more directly east to vast level forests that merge into or overspread the "Great Swamp" that lies along and is of equal extent with the Bay.

V.

To the south-east, across the Yarra-Yarra, is the Public Garden of Melbourne, one of the most interesting localities belonging to the town, and one which will long afford a beautiful testimonial to the taste and good sense of its leading inhabitants. Indeed, both in this and in the laying of its streets, the Melbourne fathers appear to have been guided by a prescience of its golden destinies. It was not without a sense of shame that I asked myself why has none of our great cities at home a public garden? (for the green at the foot of Boston Common is but a flower-pot in comparison.) Here was a new town, in a remote colony, never heard of till the gold discoveries, and yet its people had a garden, an ample space—three hundred acres at a Yankee guess—filled with rare trees, shrubs, flowers, evergreens, cacti, &c. from all parts of the world as well as those peculiar to Australia—enclosing a wide marshy lagoon half covered with reedy brake and populous with waterfowl—in a most beautiful situation—its walks all open to the public—a spot where no one can walk without growing more sensitive to the beauty of nature, and acquiring a taste for healthful and natural excitements, instead of the hurtful and factitious—one which would be a curiosity in any of our oldest and richest towns, and which would prove a greater attraction to inland visiters than any that most of them possess, and a natural antidote to the only vice we are afraid of:—all this the Melbourne citizens had, while we have been ornamenting only a few cemeteries and cultivating the single virtue—a plant sickly and unfruitful even when brought to maturity in our northern climate. I confess the first visit to Melbourne Garden humiliated me as much as it interested. I half-doubted if the star of civilization had not risen in the South before it began to culminate in the West. But this is growing didactic.

It was my first Sunday after arriving—a raw misty day; the uncomfortable sitting-room of the inn was deserted; I was alone, chilled and dispirited, without books, and unfit to appear at church. Of the country around, I had seen nothing. I had heard of the Garden, and more to weary myself and kill time than in the expectation of being interested, I set off through the muddy streets in that direction. Though the day was so unpleasant, there was quite a crowd of well-dressed people crossing the bridge—chaise carts, horsemen, and all sorts of characters passing to and fro between the city and Canvasstown. The view from the bridge includes the busiest portion of the city, and the whole of the shipping of the smaller class with which the river is filled below the dam. The incessant clang of the chimes of St. Peter's Church, to my ears, apart from its associations, very disagreeable, as well as the manner of riding, most of the horses being trained to go at a canter, and other numberless little differences, were no less observable on this day than any other. Still, with all their tearing, clumsy energy of movement, most that I met wore open English faces, and appeared as they do on Sundays in New as well as Old England. They looked more domestic than the multitudes one sees in the vicinity of New York at such times—and as I threaded my way among them I was conscious of an old fashioned home feeling—a half-awakened reminiscence of ancient Sundays in the country in Massachusetts.

Leaving the bridge, I passed two or three large enclosures containing long rows of small tenements appropriated to "Houseless Emigrants;" these belong some to the Government, some to the Emigration Society, and some to the Wesleyans, and probably other associations; they afford some accommodation for lodgers at a shilling a night, and for poor families and females—of course they do not lack tenants. Turning to the left beyond these, I walked on over the open hill. The grass was smooth and green, though not turfy, the soil being generally dry and hard, or wet and slippery. The Public Garden lies between and around a valley running up between two long swells or alluvial rolls of land, one of which I passed over and around, to the entrance on the side of the other. From the upland, the picture of the Garden, with its marshes and prevailing dark green foliage, is singularly imposing. I wish I could give an idea of the effect of the strangeness of the vegetation, both in and around it, to an altogether unaccustomed eye. The gum trees at a distance have the effect of a stately open forest—an old poetic wood, with broad shadows and sunny glades, and clouds of verdure, high and swelling, and "echoing walks between"—such a wood as we sometimes see in old paintings or in views of ruined castles, where there are herds of deer reposing, or Diana and her train are coursing in the moonlight. They realize to the eye the ideal forests of Mrs. Radcliff, or if one is more cheerfully disposed, the classic environs of Belmont, where Lorenzo and Jessica sat together. The trees standing far apart on ground as smooth and green as if it had been laid by a roller, there being no frost to break it, and no undergrowth whatever, the foliage of small Willow like leaves not beginning till twenty feet or more from the ground, and then rising with a goodly outspreading stature—the combined effect, when seen from away is superb.

But distance lends enchantment. Near at hand, the gum tree is as unsightly as in distant masses it is beautiful. The huge trunks all appear dead; the thin bark hangs in shreds upon them, and they are cracked, gnarled, bleached, full of decayed crevices, unpicturesque nodosities and tuberous contortions. Their trunks and limbs have but one character, with unimaginable variations, of ugliness. They grow like enormous weeds, without symmetry, and without stateliness, in great shapeless trunks rising upwards in potato-like forms thirty feet or less, then sprawling into crooked and equally shapeless branches,—and all ending suddenly in shoots and leaves quite too small for fair proportion. If they were straighter, they would resemble trees in very old wood cuts; if their trunks were smaller they would be like bushes; as they are, their upper portions appear like parasitical after-growths, engendered upon the half-decayed ruins of larger trees. The shoots radiate outwardly in umbrella-like clusters, ending in the foliage which from afar seems so grandly massed, but from beneath is seen to be thin and scrubby. This description will answer for most of the forests inland on the roads to the diggings. Never was there a greater misnomer than to call it "The Bush;" it is much of it composed of the white and red gum tree, and if it were not for the mud, might be traversed by carriages.

In the Black Forest, which lies among the spurs of Mount Macedon, fifty miles to the north-west, about half-way to the Mount Alexander diggings, the growth is closer, and there is more variety in the woods; but even here the growth is by no means dense, as in the forests of our Northern and Middle States. On the heavily timbered mountain ranges also the gum trees grow straighter and larger, sometimes averaging more than a hundred feet under the branches; but the undergrowth is never thick. Besides the gum, there are box, ebony, Australian pines, she-oak as it is called, and many more, all having in their growth and foliage the singular look of dreariness and antiquity peculiar to the southern portions of New Holland. The she-oak and pines grow about Melbourne in the vicinity of the Garden and elsewhere. They are not so large as the gum, and their bark and trunks resemble the fir and cedar. The former has for leaves thin clusters of dark green, dry, filaments, a foot long, like very coarse grass, and at a little distance looks savage enough. I could never see it without thinking of kangaroos and boomerangs. The sound of the wind through it was like whispers from an old world, "out of space, out of time." In almost every one the tea-plant, a sort of Australian mistletoe, had established itself and mingled its dark willow-shaped leaves with the clusters of filaments that stand out like quills upon the fretful porcupine.

All these woods are useless for timber, and they are so hard and cross-grained that they are not easily cut for fuel. The red gum is principally used for that purpose in Melbourne. It is too crooked to lie still when corded, and is sold usually in little conical loads at three and four pounds sterling for what might perhaps make half as many cord feet. It burns slowly, in a smouldering fire, but gives out much heat.

The Garden contains, I presume, specimens of all the indigenous trees and shrubs, as well as many from the East Indies and from other continents. I supposed those most frequently occurring to be the natives. Nearly all were evergreens; or were at least in full leaf in the winter month of June. The most curious were probably from northern regions of the continent, or from the neighborhood of the great swamps, which occupy a large space on the southern coast, and of whose extent it is difficult to form an idea. One to the southward of Melbourne, on the right of the Bay coming up, is sixty miles across; into others great rivers from the interior flow, and lose themselves without ever finding an outlet. Conceive the legions of mosquitos, frogs, poisonous snakes, lizards, and thousand noxious nameless things—the acres of pelicans, cranes, ducks, swans—the air that must brood over such a tract! Out of these impassable morasses spring myriads of rushes and reedy plants, and tall dense underwoods unknown in drier regions; and around their margins and on their quaking oases, stand stately groves, covered with dark unchanging verdure, and realizing in their forms the solemn romance of this wildest region on the earth's surface.

The Garden contains such a morass—not on a very small scale either. There are long walks around it, and it is fringed with cany bushes, through the openings of which it appears half covered with reeds. From around the hill where it may be overlooked, it is seen to be peopled with wild fowl, mostly a species of small duck, which swim very rapidly, and with a movement as if they were walking on the bottom; they could not even quack, I observed, in a natural manner. There were also other fowl of whom I caught occasional glimpses in the reeds, and who every now and then startled me with their hoarse outlandish screams. In an enclosure on one side of the lake were some black swans, confined there by a paling, and their wings clipped, in order to prevent them mixing among smaller water-fowl, with whom they do not live happily on account of incompatibility of temper. Their bills are bright red; they sit gracefully on the water, but their long, slender necks look almost snaky.

I was most interested by the trees, of the strangeness and beauty of which no description can convey an idea. It was not the season for flowers, and there were few in bloom. There were roses, however, and I trespassed so far as to pluck in one walk a sprig of verbena. The botanical labels were attached to the trees and plants generally where not torn off, and doubtless gave much useful information respecting them; but scientific knowledge in that branch is reserved for its professors, and for young ladies, to whom a fair acquaintance with it may be an extremely graceful acquisition. But I could gaze upon the trees, many of which would be at home the rarest exotics, and feel the poetry of them without knowing their names, or their family history. They were of many singular forms. Some were twisted and covered with fine long hair-like yellow foliage; others were piny or with cedarn leaves; some were close round masses of soft furry green, like huge asparaguses—some high, and yet as thick as box. One of the most beautiful species had leaves like the catalpa, but smaller and darker, and it stood up with its leaves outspreading in symmetrical layers, in the form of an inverted top or rounded cone, seeming to challenge the world to produce a more perfect specimen of that variety. There were many of this sort, all with the same character of rare elegance. I observed every visiter of the few that were in the Garden, stop to look at them. They were by no means lively; their forms were too purely graceful and withal too dark to wear a cheerful expression. Their beauty was that of high-bred Spanish ladies, or rather that of the music of Donna Anna in Mozart—noble, tender, serious, lovely.

The picturesque effect of the Garden was very impressive. The fine slopes of the long valley looking towards the town, the sickly fens and lake overshadowed by the verdurous hillsides, covered with paths with flower-beds and trees such as above described; around the Garden the lordly gum trees filling up the distance towards Richmond and St. Kilda, and half embosoming many beautiful English villas and cottages—compose a landscape as strange as it is striking. In the flower season it must be much more magnificent than in winter. I may be peculiarly sensitive to the language of inanimate nature; I believe she "never did betray the heart that loved her," though I could never find in her that perfect consolation which the poet promises. But that she excites my mind, and tears it from the contemplation of past ills, "rash judgments, and the sneers of selfish men," and fills my spirit with new capabilities, as well as amuses me for the moment, I believe as potently as Wordsworth could set it forth. I shall never forget the glimpses the Garden afforded me of the infinite variety and beauty that there may be here upon this common sensible earth, or how insignificant my own little experience of life seemed to me as I walked among these wild and glorious forest trees of an unexplored continent. The sombre day, the serious landscape, the wondrous evergreens, the lofty park, the sense of ancientness and remoteness, combined with the evidences of home like refinement—I think I feel it yet. I feel with what a mighty tread the footsteps of English civilization advance over the earth. I think too of the ages that had swept over these wild valleys before they heard the sound of an English voice;—and I feel as Adam might have felt in the primeval garden, before the immediate presence of the Creator. I am alone—the old affections have passed away—my former life is a dream—nothing is left but a sinful soul, that is soon to be called to the judgment. *Kyrie eleison!*

VI.

The climate of Melbourne in the winter months, though not without some unpleasant weather, is in general exceedingly fine, and to persons in good health, it must, I should suppose, be invigorating. There were many days in June when a fire was needed, and very many uncomfortable by reason of rain, mud, and dusty winds. But the cold, though disagreeable, chilling one through and through, did not take root in colds; those who are obliged to encounter it as thousands were, almost unprotected, will at first give themselves up for lost, and very soon wonder at their impunity. Either the air lacks the cold imparting quality, or the changes are too sudden to permit it to act. It certainly has a dryness even in its very wetness. When it rains, the sidewalks are soon muddy, the crossings overflowed and unfordable by people on foot; in a few hours the wind will shift, the sidewalks will be like porcelain, and a fine dust will be blowing. The nights are much warmer during the fore-part than towards morning. With all this there are many beautiful days, Indian summer-like in temperature, and with to the eye very much such a veiled atmosphere, though it is much more bracing. On such days I was charmed with the landscape.

Some of our passengers who came to avoid bronchial and pulmonary diseases at home, were much discouraged at first; but we heard that most of them took courage. This is, I believe, the general experience. But notwithstanding what was said, and that I, who am as subject to cold as an ordinary mortal, escaped, I think no one who feels anxious about his lungs ought to expect benefit from such a climate. The very dryness of the air, while it exhilarates and braces up the body, draws also upon its vigor. It seems to withdraw its moisture and wither it up. Most of those who go there from other climates, and who are not unusually robust, look worn and fatigued after a few seasons; their limbs drag, and their voices retreat to the back of their heads, and are like those of men talking in dreams; their hands are cold, their skins enamelled. This effect is common enough to be generally observable. Others there are whom the climate seems to have strengthened and made to grow like the gum tree, evermore coarser and uglier. And there are robust Englishmen in the prime of life, and men of adventure, captains and travellers, independent of climates ; and Englishmen, too, who in point of physical energy make ours appear almost an inferior race. The general mass of the English population exhibits anything but feebleness, and proves every thing but that the climate is unhealthy. But this must be owing less to the climate than to the habits of living, inherited and local. The mother country is an excellent nurse to robust children, and a colonial life keeps up strength and vigor where they exist. To an American also, who is accustomed to see people aim in public at elegance and the attractions of beauty, as our men and women do, however wide they may come of their mark, the look of an English town, where the men endeavor rather to look strong and the women dignified, their natural advantages in these respects will appear magnified, and he will begin to fancy himself among a race of giants. This was at least my experience in Melbourne. But Melbourne then held a floating population of "swells" of the heaviest order, assembled from all Christendom. On comparing notes with sundry English as well as Americans, we all found that our ideas of human expansion were daily enlarging—that London or all Scotland could produce nothing which could top the impudence of sundry "new chums" who were daily arriving. One, who took the Royal Hotel by storm, and awed the entire breakfast table into admiring silence, with eloquent thunder, strangely *h*aspirated, was in three days working on the streets. Of course it was not easy to distinguish between this class and acclimated residents.

But all residents agreed that winter and its mud was the pleasantest part of the year, and incomparably more endurable than summer and its hot winds and dust. The hot winds at Sydney are described in Wilkes; they are experienced in the same manner at Melbourne. They blow from the North, and last from one to three days. During their continuance, the air is at a suffocating dry heat; the grassy plains around the town often take fire spontaneously; business is suspended, and houses shut up as close as possible. It is not easy to face the currents of wind that blow down the north and south streets. Dust gathers in a few hours upon furniture in closed rooms, and on the faces of sleepers, to an extent almost incredible; one gentleman told me that he had waked with it covering his face like a mask, a quarter of an inch thick! But this is only occasional. The general summer weather is more tolerable. The mosquito and flea population of Melbourne, however, is numerous, intelligent and enterprising. In the bush and at the diggings, the place of the former is supplied by flies, who come in swarms almost equalling those that vexed Egypt in the fourth plague. They are unbearable at the diggings without veils; the thin coats of the people who walk in the sun will be so covered with them that the backs will seem quite black. They are large, like our horse-flies, and small like our sand-flies; and are almost fatal to unprotected eyes, producing an inflammation or opthalmia that ends in permanent weakness or loss of sight. The only relief is that they do. not pursue their avocations, or volitations, by night.

At that season the country and forests are parched, and the soil so sunburnt and indurated that carriages may travel for hundreds of miles in any direction into the bowels of the land, as upon a macadamised road, and without the slightest impediment. Indeed it is usual to travel at that season, and for most of the year, by compass, through the wide forest country between Sydney and Melbourne.

The sheep and cattle stations of the farmers inland are somewhat like plantations in the South-West, though but little of the immense grassy plains in which they lie is under cultivation. The herds and flocks number often many thousands, and are attended by shepherds, who must lead a lonely life compared with that of our farmers. As the occupation has been and still is the natural channel for the industry of the colony, and is not very laborious or difficult to get on with, it becomes the last resort of immigrants who have left home with far other expectations. The private history of the Australian shepherds, Hoosier-like as many of them appear, would doubtless form a strange volume. This indeed might be said of the gold-seekers, with whom I believe the love of gain is a less frequent motive than the wish to escape the thorn of some sad experience. It was a common saying in Melbourne that women sent more to the diggings than gold brought there. Such is the wickedness of woman. Still, for all that, we do not utterly despise her.

The horses, and bullocks, as the English call them, instead of cattle or oxen, one sees about Melbourne, are generally an extremely ill-looking and apparently ill-fed and overworked portion of the animal kingdom. The horses stop, give out, and decline going any further, or as the word is, "balk," or "jib" in Melbourne with a frequency quite noticeable. They generally exhibit in their forms any thing but the fruit of good living or careful grooming. The vehicles they have to draw are mostly a species of chaise cart built for a single beast, with a body like a huge wooden knife tray, perched on springs like a baker's cart, and having a front seat for two, and a back one or two side back ones for two more. These may be better than our old cabs, but the roads and streets are much worse, and the poor horses suffer. Hay in the city is worth from thirty to forty pounds per ton, and a saddle horse costs from forty to fifty pounds; the expense for keep is about seven pounds per week. Bullocks can be had for forty pounds per yoke. Their yokes have usually bows made of round three-quarter inch iron, which must gall the neck cruelly; they are driven in immense teams, with whips twenty feet long, and clamor and needless noise, to Colonial ears delightful—to mine not.

The escort horses are no better than those in general use. But there are now and then fine animals belonging to private gentlemen, who evidently pride themselves on their turn-outs. I am not horseman enough to know what may be its advantages; but the English mode of riding, rising in the saddle, with short stirrups and great apparent effort to get on, strikes an American as rather jockey-like than becoming. Every one rides who can, and there are always plenty of horsemen in the streets; the state of the roads and streets rendering the indulgence of the national taste a matter of necessity. All riders are provided with heavy whips, loaded at the ends of the short staves, with with hammer-like heads of brass or iron—formidable weapons to look at, but unreliable, one would imagine, as a defence against the pistol.

Mutton and beef are, of course, the meats most consumed. The joints and cuts look well in the butchers' shops on Saturday evenings, displayed in the London fashion; but it was a common remark that they were of coarser texture, and did not possess the full flavor of similar meats at home. They do not come very high; a good cut of roast or boiled, could be had at the chop houses for eighteen pence, or three shillings New York money; and if one patronized a certain zinc shanty on the market-place, yclept the "Hedgers," acertained by the author hereof to be the establishment affording the most and best cooked food for the least money, he could have a vapor bath thrown in, the confined unporous cabin being always crowded at the dinner hour to bursting. I had, however, a peculiar satisfaction in feeding there; the landlady was a grand specimen of a portly Englishwoman in the Siddons style, and entertained a noble estimate of the powers and capacities of the human stomach. I am sure she took a motherly pleasure in seeing her customers eat. She had a liberal eye and an open hand; she might have sat for Ceres, or the impersonation of Abundance. There was with her always plenty and to spare, and no niggardly glances to poison enjoyment of it. A plate of soup was a dinner; of rump-steak pie, reminding me of Scott's venison pasties, it was a fortified mountain where you might march up your forces, effect a breach here and there, and plant your flag on the outworks, but could seldom raze the citadel. Blessings on the woman. I sigh when I think how cruel fate has parted us forever!

There are good fish to be had in the Melbourne market; at the Royal we had occasionally a sort of perch broiled for breakfast, which was very good. Pork is also served in its usual forms, though it is not so much eaten as beef and mutton, and costs more. The vegetables I saw in the market looked well, particularly the cauliflowers. There were enormous carrots, nearly a yard long, and stout in proportion. The onions were oblong, squeezed, perhaps, into that shape in growing through the adhesive soil. There were also huge potatoes from New Zealand and Adelaide, but they were seldom free from the rot. The few turkeys and fowl did not promise much. Wild duck, and other game fowl, were often hawked in the streets; I remember seeing a boy with a brace of black swans.

But almost everything animal as well as vegetable of native growth, has some little oddity about its shape, as if it had run wild in this new continent. Oysters, such as only Englishmen could eat, were hawked in and eaten raw from baskets, at six shillings or more per dozen! Even the shrimp, sold at five shillings a quart, had a young lobster look. I saw frequently opossums brought in on the shoulders of sportsmen; they resemble raccoons, only that they are smaller and grayish. If the inhabitants can ever persuade themselves to eat what Frenchmen eat, they may procure from the great swamps and marshes an ample supply of frogs, which are said to grow in those locations, almost as large and loud-voiced as oxen. Our New York emigrants will be catching and broiling them—their gourmand fellow-citizens at home, have long esteemed frogs very delicate and chicken-like food.

While the Albus lay at Port Phillip Heads waiting for a wind, we pulled ashore one day near the light-house to explore the country. Our Captain and most of the seven gentlemen, my fellow passengers, being good shots, considerable execution was done among the birds, on and near the beach. The party bagged three or four, besides frightening several flocks of swans that were passing over out of distance. Each one differed from the others; one was half as large as a duck; another, something between a pigeon and a patridge in size and flight, was of a dark color, except a small spot of the brightest green and gold in the middle of its wings; most of them had the albatross bill, and all were probably birds of the water or the shore.

The beach was long and narrow. Behind it lay a wide lagune ten miles up and down, and nearly as many across, bounded by level swamps. It was as calm as a looking glass, and was dotted over with water-fowl, which were constantly flying from it overhead towards the bay at sunset, when we pulled back to the ship. While ashore, three of us who had no guns, came rather unpleasantly near meeting with an incident. We had left our companions on the beach, and walked around by some pilot houses or huts, to the light-house on the bluff, at the end of the point, looking seaward. We had hardly reached it, and were standing a few steps beyond the light-house enclosure, when there was a sharp report not far off, and a bullet whistled apparently within six feet of our heads! We had just received a surly reply to a civil remark, from a man sawing wood—had met several ugly-looking rascals, and seen other circumstances extremely unfavorable to the existence of a high standard of social morality—of course we retreated. On passing a shanty that stood on the bluff at no great distance we encountered two pilots, one of whom had a rifle, which he had, to clean it, he said, just discharged upon the ground; showing us the spot, which was in a line with himself and the place where we had been. But I had doubts; the man's eyelid quivered a little; however, at the worst suspicion, he could only have intended to discourage us from future walks in that vicinity. But it was an "incident," almost; the second indeed we had that day, for D.'s fowling-piece had previously gone off in his hands, in the cabin, sending a charge of shot through a panel, from behind which the second steward had but just moved. It was the merest accident in the world that we escaped, for we were all standing and sitting close around. But we did, and were thankful for it. I, for one, have objections to being shot any where, and particularly at Port Phillip. It would have been an ignoble end. Let me die where I can show my friends, that I go, not "like the galley slave, scourged to his dungeon."

The point where we walked was partly overgrown with trees, chiefly of the gum species, and around the low land and toward the beaches with thickets of underwood, the most luxuriant and beautiful imaginable. We saw Corin and Phyllis walking there at no great distance. But I hunted in vain in every direction for a stick which I might cut as a memento. Neither tree or bough produced aught but crooked, hard, and at the same time weak, half-rotten twigs. The ground in many places was overrun with mangrove and tea-plant creepers to the depth of several feet. In the warm season the pilot who brought us down said the place was overrun with deadly snakes, which were in such numbers that no one dared walk out after nightfall. He told stories of their chasing people and all that—a Connecticut man, too, strange to say; still I should avoid the men ashore there sooner than the snakes. Snakes do not sport rifles.

The range of elevated land called Arthur's Seat, on the other side of the Bay, was said to be full of kangaroos;—but I saw none at Melbourne, and imagine they are not often hunted in the vicinity. At the diggings they sometimes stray in among the encampments, and are taken without much difficulty. Those who had seen them told me that the accounts of their fleetness are by no means exaggerated. They use their short fore feet in springing, but alight on the hind. No dog can overtake them going up hill. The largest species are about from four to five, and even six feet high, as they sit or stand on their haunches, and weigh from two to three hundred pounds. The hind quarters, which are the only part used for food except by the natives, who eat anything, contain three quarters of the weight and strength. There is another species weighing from forty to fifty pounds, and many inferior ones, down to kangaroo rats and mice and moles, all of whom are marsupial, wearing pouches, and shaped like the large species. I know not how it is, but these animals always seem to me, like the trees and plants of Australia, to be the remnants of some far gone era of the earth's history—links in the chain connecting the living world with the fossil. The very configuration of the land, the scarce perceptible movement of the plains, the undisturbed composure of the mountains—all nature has the look of having slept since the Creation; it seems to have brooded over the past, and to be now, not fully awake, dreaming of things to come.

Besides kangaroos, the emu, or Australian ostrich, is not unfrequently seen in the neighborhood of the diggings and within fifty miles of Melbourne. The forests in the immediate vicinity contain a variety of beautiful little paroquets and large cockatoos and birds of paradise. In general the birds are less remarkable for song than for plumage. There is among them, however, a sort of magpie, and another singularly-voiced songster is quite common, and known all over the country as the "laughing jackass." A single one of these produces an infinite deal of noise. He salutes the miners in the morning with a bray like a donkey, followed immediately by a series of loud silly laughs, not all alike, but as if half a dozen jolly simpletons were laughing together. The likeness is said to be so natural, and so apparently hearty and spontaneous, that the hearer can hardly forbear joining in the chorus. Six miles is the incredible distance at which it is said this happy mortal makes his mirth audible. If he can be taught to let himself out at the right places, he will be invaluable to future Australian comedians. But he must first learn, like Goldsmith's friend on the first night of "She stoops to conquer," to take his cue from some Australian Johnson, who may be a long while coming.

I saw a few of the native savages in the streets of Melbourne. They are well described in Wilkes. They are clad in blankets and trousers much like the Indians we see at home. Their skins are deep black, hair straight, eyes deep set and restless, bodies thin, legs bowing outward, and like two bent sticks; altogether they are ugly and diminutive, jealous apparently, but not wanting in intelligence. I know not where Col. Mitchell saw the "brawny savage" hunting alone, whom he watched unobserved, and so picturesquely describes. Probably only the meanest and most degenerate visit the cities. They often come about the mines and exhibit their corrobories or wild dances, and their skill in throwing the spear and boomerang. I take some pride in having been compelled to believe that the accounts of what they can accomplish with the latter weapon are not exaggerated. They can throw it with great force and unerring certainty, and can make it crook its flight, and even cause it to return to the thrower. *How* they do it we cannot account for, any more than the showman could give the true reason for the penguins walking into the water up to his neck and turning round and walking out again. The naked fact must be believed, however, if any credit is to be given to human testimony.

"At length did cross an ALBATROSS,
Thorough the fog it came ;—"

VII.

It was not my fortune to meet Mr. Micawber or his distinguished son, Wilkins Micawber, Esq., in Melbourne; though I encountered many who had evidently formed themselves upon the senior gentleman's model; whose every-day conversation might almost have sprung from his own eloquent lips, or emanated from his facile pen. The speech of the English Commercial Traveller, alias Bagman, will doubtless one day become the universal language. The bagman penetrates into all regions, however remote, where sales can be effected at a remunerative commission; his object is to effect such sales; through him the producer is not a producer only, but the maker of his market. He manufactures; the consumer consumes—but not fast enough; the commercial traveller finds occupation in cramming him. He, in fact, produces the consumer. He combines; he separates; he gluts the market; he drains it; he bulls; he bears; he elevates; he depresses—all the while calculating his per centages in a little pocket-book. He is ready to operate in any description of property, personal, real, or choses in action; coals, Colt's pistols, books, brickbats, bullocks—he knows of a "party" who holds them for a sum certain, and who will, if pressed, even fall un-certainly for the sake of a cash transaction. This word "party," is the bagman's shibboleth—his talismanic word without which his whole species would vanish into the elements. With him, individual men or women are not persons; he knows and thinks of them only as "parties."

This word, which is in universal use in Melbourne, and which I observed to be used in the same way by new arrivals from Glasgow, Liverpool, and London,* sounds oddly enough to ears unaccustomed to the jargon of trade. A man or woman is a "party," in Melbourne; and vice versa:—the words are used interchangeably. "Excuse me, I was to meet a 'party' at ten—a gentleman from Sydney." "What 'party' was that you were walking with this morning?" (meaning what young lady.) "You recollect, Mr. Jones, the 'party' I introduced you to. " etc., etc. The associa-

* And by Dickens, writing in his own person. Query, is it from the

tion, of the word are extremely picturesque. I thought of substituting it in the poets; as for example:—

> "He was a party, take him for all in all,
> I shall not look upon his like again."
>
> "His life was gentle; and the elements
> So mixed in him, that Nature might stand up,
> And say to all the world, *This is a party!*"
>
> "What a piece of work is a party?" &c.
>
> "Parties of all sorts take a pride to gird at me."
>
> "Of party's first disobedience and the fruit."
>
> "A party's a party for a' that."

There are no viler words in any language than those introduced from the forms of law and commerce. In this particular one there is something so suggestive of contracts and bargaining, as well as such a want of definiteness, that it is singularly unpleasing.

There are many others in the Melbourne vocabulary, some of which I heard for the first time from Yankees, on the voyage out; for instance the word "chum," which used to be a cant word for a roommate in college, with the miners now means generally a companion—one who occupies the same tent, or is an intimate acquaintance. A "new chum," is a stranger who has just arrived; and by an old rule "new chum" is also equivalent to "greenhorn;" he is a pigeon to be plucked—an operation which they perform in Melbourne very expeditiously. A fortnight, or even less, generally prepares a "new chum" to receive other "new chums" himself.

The word "mate," also means a companion or partner, and is frequently used instead of Mr., as thus, "I say, mate, which is the way to —— street?" "My word, mate, it is true." The word is colonial, and sounds as though it might have been originally used to mean each man's next neighbor on the convict chain.

"The which?" instead of "what?" when the hearer does not distinctly understand what is said, is another vile phrase to ears of Americans. As also the never omitted phrase "mind ye," introduced in a peculiarly triumphant tone, whenever one person sets another right; as, "I was an hour riding to Collingwood." "The which?" "It took me an hour to ride to Collingwood." "Indeed!" "Ay, but mind ye, how muddy it was!" Hardly any answer to a question is complete without this "mind ye." At home we never use it except to impress a command upon children, or in a reply where we mean to be rather positive, and crowing. It would of course be ill-mannered to insinuate that there may be a spice of those qualities congenital in what the Quarterly Reviewers are fond of styling the "British mind."

But that Mr. Micawber has visited Melbourne is apparent, not so much from peculiar words and phrases, as in the manner and tone of intercourse generally. The rolling oratorical voice, loud enough in common conversation to fill an auction room; the magnifying lens of mind through which all occurrences take on a fictitious importance; the ah, in short, extremely inflated views of that gentleman in all statements respecting his transactions and business prospects, are as characteristic of the daily Melbourne walk and conversation as they were of his. You shall be introduced to a "party"—a gentleman; he asks you to dine, "and be particular to come at four." You go punctually, and find the gentleman in a tent filled with second-hand rubbish, a box to sit upon, and another for a table, up to his ankles in mud, surprised to see you, and utterly oblivious about the dinner. Perhaps he fishes up some red ink which you must sip, for it is very choice claret, (I intended to have preserved a phial of some shown me by a friend, for Mr. Barnum.) After a reasonable while, you, pretending only an accidental call, retire, thinking you have learned something. But no, every day brings fresh developments. All is unsubstantial pageantry, such stuff as dreams are made of, and the "new chum" very soon from wondering, gives in to the deception and becomes himself an adept. Language retreats completely away from facts and circumstances; so that words no more represent their original sense; where "tent" stood opposite to a habitation made of turf and a few yards of canvass, speech has slid down till the thing is a "house." An "elegant cottage-residence," may have descended to a stand for a boarded dwelling with two ten-foot rooms in it. A structure much resembling one of our powder magazines, becomes a "substantial mansion." Thus in everything to which language can be applied, it has gone down, and there is no actual standard relation between words and things. It is a little awkward at first—like a Barmecide feast—but one soon falls into the manner, and it is scarcely possible to over-do it. I have not the slightest doubt, that all the nuggets exhibited in the brokers' windows in Melbourne, not the slightest doubt, "mind ye," are gold—or something else; they could hardly all be green cheese · that would be too expensive.

Of course, in such a feverish state of affairs, the whole conversation is of the town, the markets, the gold, the arrivals, the great losses and gains; and there is so much life and excitement in it, that business becomes colored with the warmth of fancy, and is no more plodding and careful, but gamesome and reckless—like playing at business. The very ones most engaged and eager in its pursuits are the readiest to be amused at the parts they find themselves acting. They laugh at the "humbug"—laugh, and keep it up nevertheless all the same. Nothing can be more ridiculous to a mate in Melbourne, than to see the new chum hurry ashore and pack away to the diggings. He gives him advice how he must proceed, and helps him to render his brief stay in the town agreeable. At first you will be disposed to think the mate a most heartless and selfish fellow, because he does not attempt to dissuade the new chum from his purpose. But do not accuse him too soon. He does in effect advise the new chum by his own example, by a generally fair statement of the chances of digging, and by informing him as to what he can expect to do if he remains in the town. That he does not go out of his way to dash at once the new chum's golden expectation, is not because he does not compassionate him in his infatuation, but because he knows there is only one cure for the complaint—the cure administered by a physician, whose remedies, if somewhat harsh, are the only effectual ones, and whose name is Experience. There is no conspiracy in Melbourne to delude people into going to the mines; quite otherwise, there are plenty ready to demonstrate the folly of it—and it is not too much to say that a person of fair perceptive abilities can hardly get through the city on his way to the mines without knowing that his chances of success are very small—that he is entering upon an expedition where thousands fail, and very few make profit. But what is the use of telling this to "parties" who have the fever on them? All such true and unexaggerated statements only aggravate the disease. Go the infected must, if they have just the means to get there. While the wind is blowing that way, human effort might as well be opposed to a gale in the South Pacific. Each one's energies are sufficiently tasked in withstanding it himself. I confess that I, who am least of all fitted for such a life, and whose tastes all incline to books and the arts and quiet, would not have been sorry to have gone up for a while with a mining company, had fortune and whole limbs permitted. It is so natural to adopt the feelings and imitate the doings of those around us.

The speculative mania has come upon Melbourne "ere she was 'ware;" and she has hardly recovered from the surprise. Thousands of her citizens, of whom hundreds could be said with peculiar truth, to have done whatever they had done of good "by stealth," awoke one morning and blushed to find it—wealth, if not fame. The town that had been for years a coarse agricultural place, all at once overflowed and effervesced with new animation. Its elements no longer cohered, but separated into a state of fluxion and transition—the crystallization which is to follow has not yet arrived. An exotic population has all at once transplanted itself here, and almost hidden and outrooted the original growth. The town has almost lost its municipal individuality; the greater part of its inhabitants are so new, so mixed-up, and so busy with their personal affairs, that they take but little interest in civic affairs.

Hence one of the things that first strike Americans, especially those from our cities, is the indifference and insincerity apparent in the discussion of local politics—the concerns of the town and colony. With all allowance for his own position, he cannot avoid thinking of the Eatanswill press when he first endeavors to fathom the views of the politicians of Australia Felix as they are exhibited in the papers. The various candidates parade their pledges and occupy columns, before the elections, in defining their positions. Never was such a display of the Micawber style —such assumption of manliness, firmness, bold defiant courage, sense of right, bluff indifference to opinion—all those qualities John admires! Whether the penny-a liners get up these things for the candidates, or they are written autographically, they are the funniest specimens of make-believe one can imagine. It is very natural that they should be so; indeed they could hardly be otherwise. It requires far more than the usual abilities of local politicians to talk like men in earnest even on questions which all feel to be important. But here, where few care what is done, provided they are left alone to make their fortunes, and where the candidates themselves cannot, if they are able men, but feel that they have not a constituency who will very warmly encourage their ambition or sustain them in the discharge of representative duty, the failure is as palpable and almost as amusing as the prevarications of Falstaff.

Mr. Micawber has also inspired the daily newspapers. No pen untrained in his school could produce leaders of such ponderosity. I smile when I think how those editors must task their ingenuity—what perfection they have attained in dilution and circumlocution! My own sentences acquire insensibly a rotundity of form as I recall the ample periods, the antiquated points, outworn quotations, and overwhelming gravity which distinguish the Melbourne press. If it be, as I suppose to a certain extent it must be, with those who have to fill so much space each day, the perfection of editorial writing, to invent indirect and circuitous modes of expressing common practical opinions—to mitigate and extinguish the flames of popular excitement by turning on a flow of language—these papers certainly exhibit master-pieces of the art. The readers who postpone their feelings and wait to see "what the paper says," will never prove a troublesome class of citizens in Melbourne; their madness will evaporate in "words, words, words."

The readers of the "London Times" delight to see speculations upon the great affairs of the world served up in the grand manner, and are not disappointed; though even there the writers not seldom overclothe the matter, and leave the dignity in such high relief that the art of its manufacture is much too apparent—at least to those who have been behind the scenes. But the thunder of the colonial press!—in comparison, theatrical thunder is an infinitely closer imitation.

But I do not forget that newspaper writing is, or ought to be, an art by itself; and it is much better to have the dignity and gravity preserved, than to have journals like some well known at home, which attain vivacity at the expense of integrity—which represent each day the shadows in the air but not the constant sunlight. It is pleasant to see newspapers treating their readers as if they respected them. In these and many other particulars the Melbourne journals have advantages. They are conducted in a dispassionate spirit. They are by no means personal. They are open. They aim at a respectable tone. They are well systematized and creditably got up. I cannot say much for their activity or judgment in giving news, foreign or domestic. But they give all, perhaps, that is wanted, and always a plentiful column of rows and penny-a-line items—the daily history of drunkenness, disease, vagabondism and crime—containing almost as much as the columns of similar matter served at the London breakfast tables, and which is omitted from our papers because nobody cares to read it.

The two principal journals are the Argus and the Herald, of which the former is commercially the leading paper, as it has the most advertising. It is conducted in the style above described, by Mr. Wilson, and is understood to be radical, and to aim at hurrying the colony into separation from the mother country. The Herald has the Government advertising, and attempts to be conservative, though it is hardly true to its position. In mere writing, its editorials are better than those of its less scrupulous rival, though not so vigorous. I meant to have preserved one of its lighter leaders about the mud and dust of Melbourne, which was very happily written and much needed. If both the journals were to unite in a war against filth, they might accomplish more to the purpose than they ever can by attempting to weaken or strengthen the arms of the colonial government. But they have only to keep, as the sailors say, "full and by." Their fortunes are made already. They are crowded with cash advertisements, and their supplies of paper do not meet the demand. Sometimes their extra advertising sheets appeared in red, sometimes in yellow. When people only have to hold their pockets open to let gold run into them, it is not likely they will go digging.

Godwin makes one of his characters claim an unquestionable superiority for English writers, on the ground that "they only of all the moderns had been touched by the genius of freedom, that they dared to utter all that they thought, and that by necessary consequence they had penetrated into the secrets of nature and laid open the recesses of mind." If instead of the "genius of freedom," whom the eloquent author rather ignorantly worshipped, since that divinity had long before emigrated to America, the cause of the superiority of English writers were attributed to that combination of qualities which the language wants a single word to express, which includes vigor and health of heart, mind and body—the just and tenacious integrity —the complete manliness—it would be more precisely true; and the same cause would account for the position which England and her colonies, and her descendant and ally, now occupy in the world. Their position is the result of the inherent and natural growth of a great family. And it is in remote settlements, peopled by those who would naturally, though from very opposite causes, be the offshoots of the stock, that the family characteristics are most apparent. The strong, the ardent, the enterprising, the weak, the too gentle, the rough, the ambitious, the unscrupulous, are all poured in together; the extremes of individual character are contrasted; the restraints of home and the beaten ways of education only remembered.

It is fortunate for Melbourne that it is under the Home Government. The colonial system of England is necessarily different from that of the United States. It is not within the scope of our government to encourage or extend special protection to emigration; ours is not an overstocked but a receiving country; it is quite enough that we stand ready to take such as are prepared to come to us. Newly arising settlements of Americans in distant territories, stand on a different footing from colonies; in fact, if it should not be so theoretically, they are obliged to begin by self-government. Of this California was an example. But English colonies are spared the disorders which there necessarily precede a regular organization. Melbourne has not been obliged to resort to Vigilance Committees, Lynch law, or any experimental and temporary modes of securing the rights of persons and things. Of course there must be comparative disquiet and insecurity in such a vicinity, but there have been less than might have been looked for, if the town had not been in an English colony, and under the rule of the common and statute law of the realm. Had all the local politicians concurred, they could never have got on better, it is probable, notwithstanding the lowness and expensiveness of the government often complained of by a portion of them. Their regulations would have wanted the *prestige* and the power of the Home Government. Quite as much delay and cost, would have attended their action, and it may reasonably be questioned if their administration would have been any wiser or purer or more efficient. The colony would have gained the empty name of independence, and Melbourne would have been by this time—a nice place to live in.

Americans, on their first arrival there, hear an immense deal of disloyalty and radicalism. The class of all-knowing talkers flatter them by pretending to look upon them as the harbingers of separation and rebellion. "You are coming," they say, "now we will be free!" Of course such extreme reformers understand as little what they wish for, as they do of the means of its accomplishment.

But it is a singular fact, that Americans do not like such notions abroad so well as at home. Just as English Radicals generally become ultra Tories after they have lived a short time in America, so American Radicals side with law and order in English colonies. They look upon government from a different point of view; they are not blinded by the feelings, the party catch words and the names of canonized political saints, that obscure their judgment at home. The words "bank" or "tariff" or "abolition," no longer excite their ire, and dethrone their reason; they can offer only secret homage to their former national heroes. They soon perceive how much more practically wise they themselves are in political matters than their new friends; and they have the same pride that Englishmen have with us, which keeps them from meddling with what they fancy to be none of their business. Besides, there is a large proportion among Americans who are accustomed to act understandingly, and are little given to aid in hastening changes which they do not feel thoroughly convinced are needful. And the men of real influence, among the American merchants, and others, are entirely given to commerce and business affairs, and want no changes but increased facilities for trade. Upon the whole, therefore, the uneasy and uncomfortable portion of the Melbourne population will find less assistance in opposition to the established order of things from Americans than they look for. The Americans are in a position of indifference. They will never interfere except against open oppression, which never can arise; but all the weight of influence becoming to them as alien residents, will be given in support of a government which endeavors to overtake the wants of an almost miraculous influx of population, as fast as that population urges measures and supplies means.

And in spite of the multitude of words, and the incessant portentous hinting of the Argus and its kindred politicians, I do not think the colony desires its independence. It will take another generation—several more, after this new infusion of the maternal blood, to eradicate the old affection. The convict spirit must die out, and loyalty survive. Very little is gained by opposing with small argument and ridicule, the high and serious part of the English character. There is a reality about an Englishman's honor, and it is backed by a strong and unyielding will. The radicals plague and puzzle his slow perceptions, but they do not vanquish him. There is something in his identification of his personal with his national feelings, not affected by his opinions upon particular measures. His nationality is in the solemn depths of his nature, along with his religion and his most earnest affections. Such a character is not easily assailable. With all the commixtion of adverse elements in Australia, it must take a long while under present causes, to alienate and denationalize the English heart—to divert the deep flow of patriotism that is so blended of many currents and so freighted with noble and proud memories into a new channel; and when it is thus diverted, if it ever should be, it will remain, as we would have it remain in our own beloved country, differently developed and directed only—essentially the same.

VIII.

The crowd in Melbourne streets is so animated, and so motley, that the town has the cosmopolitan air of an old commercial city. The illusion is strengthened by the appearance of the police, who, instead of stars or badges, wear a uniform of close fitting, single-breasted coats, of dark blue, with pantaloons and caps to match, and black glazed belts, all in the London style, which they also copy in their ways and doings. They look very much like automaton machines made to walk about with one hand in the breast, and to utter the talismanic order to "move on!" which operates at once dispersively upon any little street dispute that is accompanied with high words and fist shaking. They are a very imposing body set apart from the rest of society, to show the Queen's appreciation of the poetry of Dr. Watts:

> "Dear children, you should never
> Your angry passions rise!"

So high is the royal lady's estimation of this precept, and so determined is she to enforce it, that she has actually sent to Melbourne a large detachment of the metropolitan police of London; and evidently intends that the city shall be kept in the same order with her most peaceful towns at home. Her subjects here ought to be grateful for her care. Situated and made up as they are, a boiling multitude, in which the dregs have not time to settle or the scum to float, they could hardly have devised and carried into effective operation a police of their own, which would so soon have secured confidence and rendered their streets as safe and orderly, in the daytime at least, as those of New York or Boston. Of course everything must be taken into account. The virtue, the polished manners, the abstemious habits of our cities; and the convict population, the recklessness, the wild extremes of Melbourne. The latter town is not illuminated by gas; it is only occasionally half or one quarter lighted with oil, chiefly by the lanterns of taverns, which are obliged, I believe, to keep them. The streets at ten o'clock are almost deserted. At midnight they are sound asleep, and their slumbers are never broken by the heavy rumble of those processions which in one stillest and warmest nights so often waken our city residents to humiliating thoughts on the decay of our mortal nature. They are macadamised—not paved; and in winter, they are, oftener than otherwise, wet and muddy. All the outskirts are suburbs of tented fields, and there is an enormous population of sickly dogs.

Yet the police reporters, for aught one could perceive, had no less difficulty in Melbourne than with us, to find sufficient material for the display of their characteristic descriptions of affrays and casualities. Their chapter was composed of paragraphs even more trivial, indirect and verbose, than those which it was for a while a part of my office in other days to exclude from the columns of the Courier and Enquirer. I must give a few specimens as a sample of the important items which occupy from two to three columns in the morning papers daily:—

"A Discharge.—John Scott was yesterday charged at the City Police Court with having been drunk and attempted to rescue a prisoner. The evidence *pro.* and *con.* was very contradictory. The Mayor gave him the benefit of a doubt, and discharged him."

"Stealing a Dog.—At the District Court, yesterday, Charles Bull was charged with stealing a dog. He was remanded for further evidence."

"Audacious Theft.—Some of our Melbourne thieves do certainly get to be very audacious. On Monday last some daring fellows stole a cask of ale and a cask of porter from a dray, in one of the streets of Melbourne, in broad daylight."

"Stealing Boots.—An offence of this nature was preferred against Archibald M'Kenzie. The prosecutor in this case was a lad named Felix Lloyd, 14 years of age. He was in the employ of a person named Charles, and on Saturday night he saw the prisoner take a pair of boots from Charles' shop, and walk away with them. Mr. F. Stephen appeared for the prisoner, whom he stated to be a respectable butcher, who could have no necessity to steal a pair of boots. The case wasremanded until the following (this) morning." *Herald, July* 5th.

"Singular Conduct.—Mr. Archibald M'Kenzie, the butcher, whose case was reported a day or two since, was again placed before Mr. Stuart at the City Police Court yesterday. He was then committed for trial, but admitted to bail, for stealing a pair of boots, the property of Mr. Chard, of the Eastern Market. The proof was positive that he stole the boots; yet, on the other hand, it was as strongly proved that he was a man of property, and of previous good character."—*Argus, July* 6th.

Poor M'Kenzie! It is to be feared he stole the boots. But think of the "audacity" of the "daring" fellows who made off with the ale and the porter! Whoever they were, they secured a comfortable supply of the favorite drink in Melbourne—"half and half." (Pron. "af-naf.") Surely where such crimes make up the chief part of those which occur each day, the thieves cannot be very bloodthirsty or the town suffering for want of proper discipline.

But my duty as an impartial observer, compels me to admit that much was said on the other side; and the police were often accused by individuals, of conduct similar to that charged against them in the gracefully composed paragraph from the number of the Argus above quoted. Observe the style of the narrative—so exactly in the Shakspeare manner:—

"Insolence and Inefficiency of some of the Police.—A gentleman at about half-past six o'clock on Monday evening, was passing along Stephen-street from Collins to Lonsdale-streets. When some distance from Bourke-street, he met a horse and dray being driven by a man along the footpath. Himself and several others through the darkness of the night were in danger of being run over. He crossed

Bourke-street, and on the corner by the New Market Hotel, he saw two policemen standing, to whom he reported the affair, and requested them to arrest the man or drive him off the footpath. They at first demurred to do so, and finally refused, because they said perhaps before that time he had gone off it. The gentleman threatened to report them. A boy then came up to fetch them to remove a drunken man, and they left for that purpose. The gentleman in question remarked to them he should think it was more important to remove a horse and cart from the footpath on dark night, whereby people's lives were endangered, than it was to remove a drunken man. For this remark the brace of inefficients turned round and abused the party making it in good set terms, and threatened to take him to the watch-house, a threat they did not attempt to put in execution."

The editor of the Argus was afraid to introduce any change into the city item department of his journal lest it might be impossible to avoid the "slang" of the American press—a word which he was immediately convinced it was hardly polite to use, at least with an obvious personal implication. The police department of that journal, was understood to be in part, if not altogether, furnished by Mr. Thomas Warner, late of New York, the torpedo man, persecuted of Drury, One-eyed Thompson, and the rest—of all whose affairs, which used to occupy so much of the attention of our police reporters, one resident in New York at the time, was, and is, and hopes to remain, profoundly ignorant. Mr. Warner was civil to me on one or two occasions, and is, we shall all hope, not undeserving of success in his new calling.

The objection to such full and overdone police reporting is, that neither public justice nor public morality requires it. If the public taste calls for it, an editor ought to feel that he cannot in conscience humor such a taste too far;—

that other occupations are not altogether closed against him; that he has at the worst the more honorable alternative of beggary. If the public taste does not call for it, (and who believes it does, to the extent that some of our least scrupulous journals furnish it?) then an editor ought to feel that he is misleading it against his own interest. The truth is, it requires a higher order of intellect to supply the place of police reports by lighter gossip of the hour, which must always have character in it to make it attractive, and the editors are afraid to employ abilities which it may not be convenient to dispense with. Police items can be written by machinery; but the power to touch the manners as they rise, to gossip agreeably on the topics of the moment, to reflect the passing life of the time, comes by nature, and is a special gift to many that are often endowed with little else.

It was commonly believed that the streets of Melbourne, or the least frequented of them, were dangerous to walk in after dark, or late in the evening. We heard stories almost daily of people being "stuck up" in Flinders Lane and other localities. "Sticking up" is the phrase for robbing:—you are floundering along through the mud in the dark, and are suddenly met by a "party," one or any greater number, who tell you to stand and deliver your money, or they will insert a knife into your person; you indulge the party, of course, and continue your walk—you have been "stuck up." Out of the city, on the road to the diggings or elsewhere, you may be stuck up at any hour of the day; and such little interruptions to the progress of travellers were said to be by no means uncommon, though becoming rarer. I am inclined to believe the stories of them to be somewhat exaggerated. In our western cities, Louisville and Cincinnati, years ago, there were always reports of similar outrages, and there were quarters where it was thought one could not walk after nightfall without hazard of his life. But the young men of that day did not pay much attention to such reports; nor were they much afraid, as I remember, to walk wherever they pleased. Beyond disturbing the slumbers of watchmen, it is certain that very few misadventures ever came to the knowledge of the public. So in Melbourne, I observed that the stories of "sticking up" were exceedingly vague. Nobody that I knew had ever been "stuck up," or knew any one who had. For my own part, and I am by no means brave, and quite incapable of defending myself, I walked late at night in returning from calling on acquaintances, and looked in at all sorts of places to see life, and was never molested. I remember coming from the outskirts one evening through what should have been a bad neighborhood, and stopping at a tavern where a large room full of men and women were dancing Irish jigs to the music of a blind fiddler—a jolly party, and rough enough to look at, but too merry to be meditating robbery and murder. I was careful, however, when it was very dark, to take the middle of the street. That robberies frequently occur, is very probable; but when they are so generally anticipated, almost every one goes armed, and perhaps it is well that the danger of them should be a little exaggerated.

Besides the foot police, who are always seen in the streets, there is a small detachment mounted, who are on duty chiefly in the night-time. At the diggings there is also a much more numerous mounted police, who are the chief reliance for the maintenance of order among the miners. The roads are protected by the various companies of escorts, who number several hundreds, and who travel up and down in parties of from eight to fifteen. I knew several of them, young Englishmen or Scotchmen of respectable families, who were glad here to accept even this rough employment as a temporary resort. They are obliged to groom their own horses, and do not change their clothes on their journeys. The life is quite a different one from that to which many of them were accustomed at home—but they are young and strong, and do not appear to dislike it. They have a barracks of sheds and tents in the beautiful St. James's Park towards Richmond, where the nursery maids who walk that way may sometimes behold them sauntering idly about in their uniforms of blue with white facings, and riding sticks to tap their long boots with—wingless angels, condescending to resemble ordinary young gentlemen. How many fond aspirations they drag with them through the miles of sloughs between the city and the gullies of Ballarat and Bendigo, can only be conjectured. I have heard Yankees offering to take a contract to stick up any of the escort parties for a very moderate compensation; and at an odds against them in numbers which made the offers look like boasting, as it doubtless was. The escorts wear swords and carbines slung at their backs; as they canter through the streets, and *teeter* (no other word but this New England one expresses the motion) up and down on their saddles, they look rather formidable. It would not be so easy to rob them;—and ——— would fight, I am sure.

There is doubtless not a town or city in the world where English is the principal tongue spoken, that shows so great a variety in its streets as Melbourne. The English are chiefly from London, and the great manufacturing towns, and from the northern counties and Cornwall—but no untravelled American can undertake to place them. There are great rough specimens about the horse and cattle markets that look as if they had walked out of old farces. Thronging the auctions are others of a different mould—all, however, mighty men in manners—noisy, impetuous, eloquent—everything the reverse of cautious in appearance, yet each thoroughly posted in his department, and usually in nothing else. To characterise the Colonial manner in a word, as it appears to an American, it is overbearing. There is little attempt at suavity or "soft sawder," but a great effort to do the grand. In speech, in walk, in ride, in costume, in air, in everything, the latent fundamental idea is to overcome, rather than to circumvent or attract. They use the two-handed sword and the downright blow.

The style is impressive at first, but in the matter of trade at least, the clear-headed and more wary American is not likely to suffer. John fights well according to his system, but Jonathan is quicker and more fertile of expedients. He is insensible to the effect of John's eloquence and his high manner; and when it comes to the close grip in driving a bargain, they are pretty nearly matched. I doubt if either has the advantage in affection for the idol they both worship. I think one as faithful to his "pund-shilling" as the other to his "almighty dollar." Perhaps it is prejudice, but I rather guess Jonathan will be not wholly unsuccessful in the long run.

There are also representatives without number of the land that lies to the north of the Tweed, with heads as long as Burns's grace; endeavoring, with the rest, to turn the honest penny. Innocent, unsuspecting people, caring but little for worldly gear, and never looking to the main chance! It is remarkable how they get on, and still continue to lay by something for a rainy day. Already, such is the blindness of fortune, they hold a very considerable portion of the wealth of the city.

There are also Irish, wide awake to make or lose money

—it matters little which to them. The Irish, we all know, are the most meek, inoffensive creatures in the world. Hence it is, for the humor of the thing, probably, that so many of those unfortunate youths who get into rows, and are brought before the Mayor's court each morning, assume Irish names. Instead of John Smiths, and James Browns, there are always Michael Donovans, Patrick O'Tooles, and Barney McGuires, and all the rest of the Macs and the O's.

Deutchland is also represented by tobacconists and restaurants, and numerous dealers in varieties, who live on nothing, and dispose of little articles at five hundred per cent. profit, and put the proceeds quietly into their pockets and say "*wie gehts!*" "I do pretty vell—not mosh!"

I have alluded to the circumstance of there being individuals of the Jewish persuasion in Melbourne. I use the plural purposely; there are more than one. At a round guess there may be ten thousand; it would not be safe to fall much from that. There are English Jews, German Jews, French Jews, *Jew* Jews—Israelites of the Israelites. They are in swarms. There are great Jews, little Jews, rich Jews, poor Jews, fat Jews, lean Jews, dark Jews, light Jews, hooky-nosed Jews, and Jews with reddish hair. I saw American Jews, Irish Jews, even—all but Scotch or Yankee Jews, (that would be a combination and a form indeed.) *Qua* Jew, I have no more antipathy to a Jew, than to an individual of any other race. Had Providence so ordered it, I don't know that I would have entertained any special objection to being born a Jew—a Mendelssohn, for example, or even a Rothschild. I would have ran away with Jessica had I been Lorenzo; and I ever preferred Rebecca to Rowena. But the Shylocks and the Jews of Chatham street, are less to my taste; and to this class the Jews of Melbourne chiefly belong. There are Jewish bankers and merchants, however, whose respectability is undoubted. The house of Jacob Montefiore, is Jewish, the American Consul, Mr. Henriques, is Jewish by descent; and there are many more, including some of the wealthiest inhabitants of the town. But the Jews of the stalls and the second-hand shops, and the auctions, are too fond of buying and selling to please a fastidious fancy. It is generally supposed that they hold it no sin to cheat Christians, and to crucify each individual believer in the cross, afresh. There is a presumption against them; they are looked upon as from infancy *capax doli.*

I saw, by the way, several specimens of London boys, not Jewish, who had all the talk and manners of grown shop-keepers. It was marvellous how fluently they could talk. The shop phrases, the slang, the impudence,—they had the whole in unimaginable perfection. At the El Dorado, on the Market Place, where I sometimes took tea, there came one who actually took away my breath—made me marble with too much conceiving. He was Bailey, Sairey Gamp's admirer, exaggerated. The coolness with which he bullied the waiters, and boasted of his standing in the affections of the cook, (to whom he was as Gulliver to Glumdalclitch,) was astounding. But to hear two or three of them, such as he together, keeping the flash conversation, was most curious. They would run on just like men, only occasionally would come something so natural and child-like, that it was pitiful. I could not but moralize the spectacle, and think how like them we all are; how parrot-like we rehearse the stereotyped phrases of life or letters, the while our hearts are sick for the sports and the loves of our youth!

But there is a class of the Melbourne population which can only be met with in an Australian city—a class which while it impresses its presence most forcibly and unpleasantly upon a stranger, is, by its marked character, a satisfying testimony to the excellence of the English law, and the purity of its administration—a strong proof that justice, in the United Kingdom, if not absolutely unerring, does generally succeed in finding the right offenders. The convicts, or those who have been such, the "lags," as they are called, are numerous enough, and it requires but little sagacity to distinguish them. Generally they have marks by which they may be readily recognised; the high cheek bones, with gray, retreating, unsteady eyes, and foreheads villainous low. The worst of our prisons cannot produce faces to compare with those that may often be seen in Melbourne; faces which not seen under suspicious circumstances, or marked with the consciousness of guilt, for they often belonged to individuals well dressed and in respectable positions, yet told of whole generations of crime.

We seldom encounter such faces in the United States; hereditary traits are less observable, and local peculiarities and individualities wear off sooner. We seldom start, as I often did in Melbourne, before young, and in more than one instance, beautiful features, thinking almost aloud—"My God! what forbears, what a father and mother that creature must have had!" And I never saw such absolutely fearful countenances as were worn by many of the old; so coarse and livid, and with eyes that had pupils no bigger than pin-holes, out of which seemed to look devils incarnate. What an old Scotchman that was who wanted me to take lodgings with him! He might have sat for the ideal of Macbeth's "withering murder." Some of these faces were like his, the extreme of ugly and repulsive; others were cruel and cold, and full of dark meaning; others not wanting, or that had not always been wanting in beauty, and that told sad stories of suffering in the over-populated manufacturing towns. I was often reminded by them of Jane Eyre, Wuthering Heights, Oliver Twist, and the hundreds of less able novels and tales of crime of the modern school. They kept me continually alive to unwelcome thoughts. I shall never forget one young girl, with a slender figure and brown hair, and fair delicate English features, and a voice that haunts me even now. She belonged to a family lately come from Manchester, who had just set up their shanty of sheet zinc and canvass next to the tent of some of my ship companions. I never heard her speak but once; but her accents were so musical and pure, and her manner so feminine, that I fell in love with her at sight. Yet there was a something in her face, not weakness exactly, nor badness, but moral dullness, and the look of a heart that had never dared to hope, which made me inexpressibly sad. Poor creature!

All the Englishwomen speak eloquently. They have round voices, and the language flows naturally from their lips. They do not have to outgrow provincialisms, and acquire a separate speech for court occasions. In America only a few in educated families have this advantage. The rest are always endeavoring after eloquence; and they often overshoot the mark, and allow their silver-arrowed tongues too high a flight. In Melbourne I daily heard the language more naturally, directly and easily spoken by them, than I have ever heard it elsewhere, except in half-a-dozen instances. But why should I suggest any new secret of attraction to our damsels, when already———

There are some pretty barmaids in Melbourne. It is the English fashion to have barmaids. I like it. I had rather see a pretty girl any time than a cigar-smoking, tumbler-tossing fellow, with his hair greased and rolled, and soap-locked at the sides, and coiled away over his forehead. Only one is ashamed to drink vile brandy before the face of a charming young lady—at least I was. However, they don't seem to mind it, and we soon got used to it. There are plenty of girls who seem to be created to be barmaids, and that sort of thing. I made a conquest of one—at least.

Pardon the natural vanity which impels me to tell it. Going once into the Imperial, or the Queen's Head, or the Royal Oak, or some other tavern, I saw behind the bar a blooming maid, looking very cross, and evidently with her temper ruffled. What suggested it to me I know not, but I instantly, in that bland and insinuating manner, which I can sometimes assume, called for "a glass of ginger beer, cold, and with a pleasant expression of countenance, would you oblige me, ma'am?" The beauty hesitated and turned redder, and—laughed outright. I had conquered; the beauty might be behind the bar, but before the bar was the dignity. I never entered the place afterward without meeting a smile, and often an allusion to my novel request. Some writers now would go on and boast of kissing a barmaid behind a door, just as they do of their exploits in trout fishing and deer shooting. I stop here. The truth is, the English maids are rather taken by Americans. I hardly know why, unless it is the maids are so much more self possessed, and can talk so much better (I do not say that they are any prettier, mind ye!) than most of their class in the United States, that Jonathan instinctively treats them with a deference which they do not receive from their own countrymen.

For my part I have always found that servant-maids possess the common attributes of humanity. It rests me to talk with Jenny about her household matters; I like the sound of women's voices. I find it possible to gossip with the maids, and indulge the social good will which ought to subsist between men and women, without any fear of degrading myself or them. I have taken some pride in having often had them come to me for advice; and when I have been sitting lonely in number seventeen, it has been a pleasure to me to hear Margaret or Susan, coming along the passage with her armful of towels or pillow-cases, skip half a dozen of the rooms in her round in order to knock at mine, and be surprised to find me in.

But I have always been a child in some things, and shall be till I die. I reproached myself for my simplicity, while I was pained to hear, particularly in some instances, where all had seemed otherwise, that the Melbourne girls are generally looked upon as too susceptible to casual attentions and the influences of gold. It is natural that it should be so in such a population, and where there are so many more men than women.

Children are also scarce, of course. One Sunday morning, at the Royal, I heard a great outcry, and rushed down stairs, thinking what could have happened. The women had got a *live baby* in the breakfast-room, and were smothering it. They came from far and near, as we see pigeons in the street, and there was noise enough to make one think he had actually arrived at the region where the world stands on its head. The poor infant lived about fifteen minutes; they set upon him all together, and ate him entirely up!—nothing being left but some of his apparel—a cap with blue ribband, piece of flannel and napkin, exhibiting a map of the gold district of New Holland. And yet Mrs. ——, and Mrs. ——, and the Misses and maids, put on their bonnets and folded their prayer books in their hands after the most approved style, and sailed off in the sunshine, to St. Peter's Church, as coolly as if nothing had happened. Some idea may be formed of the state of crime in a town where such enormities pass unregarded.

I have mentioned the bar-maids. There are in and about Melbourne, from three to five hundred bars, taverns, wine vaults, cider cellars, or gin or ale shops, however they should be called. There may be a thousand. Perhaps one house out of every twelve, is devoted to this traffic. The bars are kept openly, not hidden, as they are in Boston, or confined to basements and bye streets, but on the street corners and in the most public places. The proprietors pay large sums for their licences, and are obliged to procure bondsmen to perform their licence conditions. I was told it costs them from two to three hundred pounds to open their establishments, exclusive of rent and fixtures.

They are kept by men and boys, girls and old women. I remember one near the Court House, where were two dames, each upwards of fifty, doing the youthful in wigs and paint. What faces they had! Their bars are furnished with pumps to draw ale, and liquors are also drawn from casks through pipes. The drinker is not suffered to pour from a decanter for himself, but is served from little pewter measures. The smallest of these, about the size of an egg-shell, holds a sixpenny-worth of brandy or gin, and is called a "nobler"—a word derived, probably, from the ring. Twice this, or a "glass," which would be a large glass with us, costs a shilling, (or two York shillings.) At the best houses, the dark brandy is perhaps as palatable a poison as the article thus vended in New York, but more frequently it is a compound of all that is nauseous and abhorred of gods and men. The practice of drinking at bars, is, of course, almost universal, though business men are not expected to have leisure to indulge in business hours. The bars must do a thriving trade The Royal one was almost always crowded. The boarders, however, did their drinking in the evenings in the dining-rooms.

What novel scenes were here enacted, no pen of mine can recount. The constant new arrivals, the jolly captains, the queer characters disguised "lags," and indefinables that used to stray in here, made it a very centre of Melbourne life. Here was a posture-master, grinding the overture to William Tell on a lost seraphim; then came fresh lots by the Marco Polo and other ships, too many to enumerate, each lot having of course to celebrate its happy arrival; there was the gigantic—surnamed the Bengal Tiger—the little,—the grand. Each one played his part as faithfully as if it had been written for him. It was as if all the greenhorns of the three kingdoms, and the States, were sending perpetual deputations here. They came and went like shadows, and said and acted the absurdities and inconsistencies of dreams. We ceased to be astonished. One evening I remember a respectably-dressed man in black boasted that he could drink his glass off, standing on his head. No sooner was it said than done—with ease too. He was a transported rope-dancer, who had not been able, it seemed, in the words of Sir Thomas Browne, to "tread lightly this funambulatory track of goodness." The champion of the light weights took the heaviest man in the company on the palm of his hand and stood him on the table. A Greenock youth had been to the theatre, where some stranger had deeply wounded his feelings by appearing to regard him as a suspicious person; it hurt him extremely. Fancy such an infant, not imbecile either, sent out by his loving father to make his fortune in the mines! But why should they not put their sons out of the way as well as dispose of their daughters at auction? There are fathers of whom much will be required—who know better, and who yet act towards their children as if they had no more parental affection than those animals which devour their young. I have heard it said, and in part believe, there are those who send their sons off to get rid of them—send them and abandon them to the mercies of the gaming houses of San Francisco, or the bar-rooms of Melbourne! But it is consoling to remember that even the wide world is merciful. The well-meaning sooner or later find friends everywhere.

Though I have put the best face upon it, I would not have it imagined that I incline to spend my evenings in this manner. I have seen rough life enough. But I had no choice; there was no repose—not so much as in the ship's cabin. Melbourne life is all out of doors, or in a crowd. One can walk, when it is not too muddy, or he can take to his bed; it is very difficult to get even a sleeping closet alone. As for myself, I must have some place of study, no matter how small, where I can look through a loop-hole upon the world, or I am like a snail without his shell. Years enough have passed for me neither to be ashamed nor vain of having in my time been more than once as forlorn in a great city as ever Johnson and Savage were in London; I never had luxuries—but I want quietness. I do not "agnize a natural and prompt alacrity in hardness." I am possessed with a gentle melancholy, and the health of my mind requires that I should be secluded when I please. "Out, John!" is my motto. I would not exchange the certainty of a few years of quiet before the last resting place, for all the gold in Australia.

The noisy confusion of Melbourne only strengthened this feeling. It would be even a pleasurable excitement if one could only escape from it at will; it would heighten the enjoyment of a snug room and old books and old music—just as the noise of a schoolroom makes the single desk in a corner the best one for study. But this was unattainable, and forms the greatest objection I should have, (and other Americans must feel more or less as I did,) to residing in such a town. No thoughtful man, or man at all sensitive, could long preserve his integrity in the utter *adriftness* of such a life.

IX.

If it were not for the incessant agitation of Melbourne, a traveller whose means or occupations would allow of his only feeling the stir remotely, and mingling in it occasionally, might spend much more time there than I did very agreeably. If he had no curiosity about the mines, and did not care to study rough manners and strange characters, there is yet enough to interest in the strangeness of the country and its productions, and there is also by no means such an absolute deprivation of society as intelligent Americans might anticipate. The growth of the city is very different from that of San Francisco. It is not a new last retreat of lawless and adventurous life, but a great colonial town, settled and principally peopled by enterprising men from the three kingdoms. The emigrants from some of our American cities cannot but have experienced no small surprise on their first arrival to find themselves in such a place. Many must have ascertained in a few hours what they would never have been convinced of at home; that their native towns and villages are not quite in the very centre of modern civilization. The articles brought there to speculate on would show this. It is at once melancholy and ludicrous to fancy the disappointments, the humiliation that must have been felt by many of my worthy countrymen who were coming to spread light, and make money out of their superior enlightenment in what they fancied to be but a dark, or at best but a twilight region. "Nothing is, but thinking makes it what it is;" and wisdom in this world goes by comparison. If many at home in all classes, even writers of books, could perceive how little, estimated by the great world's standard, is their peculiar wisdom, they might yield so far as to concede that they had not monopolized the whole of that precious acquirement. But if I deviate from the regular course of these sketches for the sake of telling unwelcome truths, I shall forfeit my insurance.

Besides the numbers of men of travel and intercourse to be met with among the crowd, there are many among the permanent inhabitants of the town, who constitute a society, or if the reader can bear the word, an aristocracy, of intelligence and respectability not inferior to that of most of the large towns in the United States. Circumstanced as they are, they are compelled to be exclusive, but their very isolation makes them very glad to welcome strangers. They feel the deprivations attending a residence in a distant colony; they wish their children to be well informed, and they are not so confident in their means of educating them as to wish to offer impediments to their improvement through society. Consequently learning, good sense, good manners, the graces of good character, in strangers, are much regarded. There is no jealousy of educated men; nor is there any special want of them; if one is compelled to labor to live, the hand is a safer dependence than the head. But if not, it cannot be doubted that there are many pleasant families, and no want of intelligent and even elegant society.

I opine this from the out-door appearance of the houses and the streets, the public institutions, amusements and doings; for I was so uncertain of remaining from week to week, and had so much else to think of, in contriving how to get home, that I confined my studies to the life and society into which my circumstances forced me. Except some walks, I "knocked about" in the street and tavern, wore a beard like an opera druid, and changed my linen—as often as the rest of Melbourne generally changed *its*. My boat was on the shore, and my bark was going to be on the sea, and that month or never I determined to be as piratical as—a book-seller. I soon discovered that the state of literature in Melbourne would hardy justify me in entering into competition with the accomplished writers by whom its public are daily enlightened, and it occurred to me that if I allowed myself to have a good time, and return home, I might contribute my widow's mite of amusement to my fellow-citizens there. For now that our country is glorious, happy, free, prosperous, united, extending, and all that, it has been decided that we must have our harmless amusement! Accordingly my views of Melbourne domestic, and social, and gentler side of life should be received as those of one whose business in the state made him a looker-on in Vienna, and who was not of the country though chance made him use it for the time. An indulger in the *dolce* FAR *niente.*

Melbourne boasts a Mechanics' Institute, which occupies a conspicuous building in an excellent situation at the upper end of Collins street. The Institute is similar in its objects, and stands in much the same relation to the gold capital that our Mercantile Library Association stands to the commercial capital of the United States. Its building contains a library, not large as yet, but exhibiting quite a collection of good books; a reading-room supplied with papers, Home and Colonial, and which has lately ordered the leading journals of America; a hall for lectures and concerts, already too small, and put to service nearly every evening, and rooms devoted to city offices. I was almost a daily visiter here, and am indebted to Mr. Paterson, the Secretary, and to Mr. Millar, the Librarian, for more than merely official courtesy. In the secretary's room, along with pieces of curious mechanism, piles of second-hand books, music, engravings, and the like, the usual rubbish of such apartments, hangs a skeleton, which I remember taking affectionately by the hand when I came away, at the same time thinking within myself, if not remarking, that I was more fortunate than my friend Bones, who had been probably a brother of my craft, that had arrived in Melbourne before the date of the Institute, and the worthy officers. Without them, I might have been by this time, grinning along-side of him.

It was pleasant to see such an Institution, in such a hurry-scurry city, so prosperous. The directors meet in the hall Monday evenings, and transact business over a good supper—an excellent regulation. I saw once a heavy roll of old Manchester Guardians in the Secretary's room —far on their way, let all cheerful and thoughtful men hope, to oblivion. In the lecture hall, were numerous pictures and engravings, cases of specimens, apparatus, busts and the like—among which latter was one of Washington, borrowed for our Fourth of July dinner, the size of life, but so drolly anglified, his children could hardly recognise him. There was the always caricatured Voltaire, whom all good Calvinists delight to execrate, and Dante, the invincible, and Shakspeare, who, if he ever resembled his popular busts, could never have been Shakspeare but by a miracle. One end of the hall was a raised platform, used as an orchestra, or place for the lecturer's rostrum. Here stood a grand piano, and here on Saturday evenings, listen ye, who think of Melbourne as a paradise of rogues, meets a little club of amateur musicians, who strive to drag the spirits of Hadyn and Mozart out of elysium. When I inform them that the performance is almost as painful as that of the Euterpians, or the Music Club of Boston, our dilettanti will understand to what an intolerable degree of civilization the other end of the world has arrived. The native corrobories, described and sketched in Wilkes, where the dancers are shewn imitating a dance of skeletons, was but a rude attempt at the refined horrors of amateur music clubs. I helped them do (for) a symphony of Mozart's, (the one in C., number four, with the beautiful andante and the bold and characteristic presto finale,) one evening, and am entitled to speak. I did not shine particularly on the occasion. The instrument was too weak. Give me a good new violin that never was touched, and a long strong bow, and I flatter myself I can hold my own with most amateurs in point of *tone*; though I am rather too conscientious about putting in all the notes, and there are those who excel me in *time*, coming out ahead in spite of all I can do. Perhaps I might not fail, however, with my coat off; or if I had had some previous training at wood-sawing. Amateurs, be it understood, play for honor, and each one as the Gow Chrom fought, "for his own hand," the world over.

There are some very good concerts in Melbourne. The advertisement of one in a paper before me, opens with the first movement of Beethoven's second symphony, followed by airs from Masaniello and Lucia, second part Zampa, Adelaide, ballads, and God save the Queen. There are not wanting good violinists, and the wind instruments from the band of the fortieth regiment, are as respectable as those in most of our orchestras. At the theatre was a German double bass player, whom I had known in Boston. Some time in June, a solo violinist arrived, whose name was like my own, and my few American friends began to fancy from his advertisement, that I was about to make my *debut*, a step higher in that branch of art, than I ever reached. I called on my namesake, found him to be from London, and about commencing business as a dealer in music, and instruments; he was amused at the coincidence of name, and what was most singular, had found near him still another namesake, a stranger to him also, as both were to me, so that there were almost a bushel of us. We called upon the third Richmond, and said "when shall we three meet again!" My artist double furnished me with the arms of the family; according to the authorities, we go back to a knight who fought in the Holy Land, and the effigies of some of our ancestors may still be seen in churches in Derby and Lincolnshire. The name is in

Shakspeare, where its possessor is attached for high treason—a gentlemanlike sort of crime. In old Massachusetts I am the fourth from the same root, and trace right back to Plymouth and 1638—more than two centuries. And I intend to shed such lustre on the name that with me shall commence for it a new era; the next ages shall date from me instead of the crusader!

The theatre in Melbourne is the amusement of the middle and lower class of its population; one sees here the squatters and shepherds—as rough an audience as ever appeared before a stage. The house is small, and all its arrangements are tarnished and soiled. The dingy light exhibits a dress circle, compared with which that of the Chatham is magnificent. The orchestra, that advanced guard in the march of art, is feeble and thinned—worn out in the battle. I could not but pity the veterans of the forlorn hope who had carried the war so far into the enemy's country. Beyond them was nothing but the pioneers—the leather stockings of the bar-rooms and cider-cellars, from whom, by the way, I heard hornpipes and reels played with a vigor and spirit, and in a truly national style, that was as characteristic and almost as difficult to acquire, one would suppose, as the style of a master. The acting was like the music. The tragedian was tall, ill-made and ugly; his throat was so long, that he had apparently tried to shorten it by tying a great knot in the middle. He was all art; he concealed nothing; his points, and voices and inflections, were all shewn wrong side out; he might have been made of wood. He ranted occasionally "a few;" when he had to speak of "walking in the shrubbery," he invariably called it "scrubbery." The heroine was worthy of him; she was the—I forbear. The play was worthy of the performers; the hero was a shepherd, and the drama evidently an inspiration of native genius.—I retired after a few scenes. The moon was shining brightly outside, and I passed along Queen street, and gazed down the valley through the wide curve of Great Burke, which will, by and by, afford one of the finest street views by night in the world.

Besides the theatre, there was Rowe's American Circus, horses, and negro singing, said to be very popular, but I did not patronize it. It is with me a whim of conscience never to pay a halfpenny to the professors of the Black Art.

There are various other amusements of a still coarser description, reflecting the lowest and most repulsive phrses of Melbourne life. But why should I particularize them?

* * * * *

My sketch of Melbourne life must end here, with the sentences written two days before we reached Callao. The following report of the first Fourth of July Dinner at the Antipodes, will make an appropriate conclusion.

[*From the Melbourne Argus and Herald.*]

ANNIVERSARY OF THE DECLARATION OF AMERICAN INDEPENDENCE.

The anniversary of the "glorious fourth," as our republican kinsmen proudly love to call the fourth of July—the day upon which the independence and nationality of the United States were first proclaimed to the world—was celebrated on Monday evening at the festive board in the Commercial Hotel.

The large room in which the dinner was given, was decorated with very good taste for the occasion, and the *coup d'œil* which it presented, reflected much credit on the Committee of Arrangements, who, considering the deficiency of suitable appliances under which they unavoidably labored, contrived to produce an effectiveness and *ensemble* in the general appearance of the room, which was very pleasing. Flags, banners, and ensigns of various countries, were gracefully displayed along the walls, and upon the ceiling. At the head of the room, over the chair, the "star-spangled banner" of the great republic, was supported on the right by the British flag, and on the left by the French tricolor. Along the sides, the colors of America and England, draped in decorative forms, occupied alternate compartments; and at the end the flags of the two great nations of the Anglo-Saxon race were intertwined, with a boquet in the centre. Along the ceiling, also, flags were festooned in ornamental fashion, uniting in a knot in the centre, from which depended a circular chaplet of flowers

At the head of the room, immediately under the American colors, was placed the declaration of American Independence, set in a frame, with a bust of Washington, bearing a laurel chaplet upon a pedestal in front. On the right, close to the British colors, were engravings of Her Most Gracious Majesty Queen Victoria, and the late Duke of Wellington. The room was well lighted; and altogether, the decoration was very effective.

An excellent band lent its enlivening strains to enhance the gaiety of the evening; and it is only justice to say that, with but one or two slight exceptions, this first celebration in Melbourne of the grand festival of the United States passed off with the utmost gaiety and harmony, and in the most creditable manner.

Six o'clock P. M. was the hour fixed for the dinner, but it was nearly seven o'clock before all the guests were seated.

The chair was occupied by J. A. Henriques, Esq., consul for the United States in Melbourne. On his right hand sat Capt. Cole; on his left, George Mowton, Esq., Penn., Vice-President. Amongst the other gentlemen seated in the neighborhood of the chair, were the members of the Committee of Arrangements, viz., Messrs. Geo. F. Train, Mass., second vice-president; J. H. Fisher, Va.; third vice-president; A. H. Ackerman, N. H.; W. B. Amy, R. I.; S. T. Hooper, Conn.; M. Ross, N. Y.; E. Lloyd Throckmorton, N. J.; E. W. Cobb, Del.; N. Rogers, Jr., Md.; O. H. Holden, N. C.; Henry Whitin, S. C.; and T. Gardner, Ga.; Also Messrs. Hathaway, U. S. Consul in Van Dieman's Land, J. Guthrie, her Majesty's Customs, F. A. Dalgety, Rev. Mr. Corrie, &c., &c.

There were about 150 gentlemen present.

The dinner, which was an excellent one—the wines and the desert being also very good,—was discussed with right good will; and on the cloth being withdrawn,

Mr. Mowton, at the request of the chairman, read slowly and with good emphasis, the Declaration of Independence, which was enthusiastically applauded at various passages, and at the close of this celebrated historic document, the applause was renewed with redoubled effect.

According to the programme of the evening's proceedings, Mr. Geo. F. Train next read the following address, from the pen of Mr. Peck, Massachusetts, who was unable to deliver it in person, as he was to sail on the day of the dinner in the Albus, for Callao. The good taste in which the sentiments of the address were conceived drew forth repeated plaudits. It is as follows:—

ADDRESS.

Countrymen and Guests of American Residents of Melbourne,—This day will hereafter be memorable as the first Fourth of July ever celebrated by citizens of the United States in this great commercial town. We who are present, will always be able to recollect with pride that, at this time, in this most remarkable vicinity, where all is bustle and resort, and a populous and beautiful city is rising around us like an exhalation, we did not forget the far land of our birth.

It is both proper and pleasant that we should assemble in this social manner, to enliven in ourselves the natural love of country, without which our souls would be dead indeed; that we should on this day, in whatever new home of our adoption, turn our thoughts back to the home of our childhood; that we should call to mind the glory and honor of our nation; her history, the illustrious men she has produced; her growth and present greatness, and hopeful future:—that we should image to ourselves all that makes our hearts swell, when we think of our native land, and the kindred and friends we have left. This is the birthday of our nation; and though now Australians, we were originally, and must ever continue to be, Americans. Never can we become alien to the great Commonwealth, whose existence dates from the day we celebrate.

Fellow countrymen, we meet here under circumstances more peculiar than those which will probably attend any similar celebration this year, the world over. We are in the van of a great immigrant expedition which is concentrating in this colony from all parts of the globe; and which has already thronged these streets with such a crowd of busy men as can hardly be found anywhere but in the oldest commercial cities. We are also in a foreign land where nothing is foreign—where we hear the accents of the tongue our mothers taught us to speak, and behold everywhere the presence of laws, and a social organization almost identical with those under which we were born. We are aware that we are foreigners, as an abstract fact,—we have not yet voted in any "town meetings," and feel greatly abridged in the exercise of the American privilege of settling the affairs of the nation; but with these, and a few local differences, all around us, is so like our cities at home, that we almost need the daily evidence of the heavens to make us believe we are at the antipodes. We have not reached the lawless neighborhood we read of; we see nothing violent; on the contrary. we are in a quietly-disposed town, under an efficient police, where a decorum prevails which, considering the numbers and adventurous disposition of the population that is pouring through it, far exceeds all reasonable expectation. We see on every hand the tokens of the existence of an indoor domestic life like that under which we were educated. But for some finer and more delicate sense than sight, we could hardly know that these were not our own countrywomen, who walk in unquestioned security, and add so much beauty to these broad thoroughfares. The look of business, amusements, the panorama of the streets—even to the very prints in the windows—all belong to some of the upper avenues of New York. And, on Sundays, the sound of the churchgoing bell is heard through an air as silent as floats over the stillest valley in New England.

In such an orderly population, we Americans, met here for the first time to celebrate the beginning of our national independent existence, wish to express most unequivocally the satisfaction we feel at finding ourselves regarded as not wholly strangers, but simply such as we are—Americans; as only not Englishmen. As men of like speech, like customs, like thoughts, and like religion with Englishmen; and whose nationality, so far as respects what at home we style the "Mother Country," and her colonies, extends but to fair and open emulation in the pursuits of commerce. In thus expressing ourselves, it will not be thought presuming to add, that though we are now under our own Government, yet we have never laid down our respect for the Head of that great nation, from whom we derive our lineage, our language, our common law and the spirit of our forms of Christian worship.

We believe that there can, by no possibility, ever come any other national feeling or hope to the wisest men of England and America, than that the two countries may remain disposed for ever towards each other as they are now. Differing policies may, in the course of events, be deemed advisable by the two Governments, but nothing will ever be more odious to the high-minded statesmen of both, than the encouragement of a petty, illiberal, ever-disparaging national prejudice. Englishmen are above it, and we are above it; it is beneath the dignity of common sense. We owe almost everything in which we are superior to England, to improvements upon, and not departures from her system; and she, we flatter ourselves, has some reason to be proud of, and in some particulars might profit by, the example of her offspring. Let us pray that Heaven will kindly send in the future such leading men to each nation as those immortal ones we have last year mourned; that the succession will be perpetual, of ministers and negotiators, who will desire to behold the two Powers united in spreading the peaceful spirit of commercial enterprise, the old law, and the old intuitive reason which is the soul of our common literature, throughout the isles of the sea, and the uttermost parts of the earth.

We do not deprecate, in these expressions, the existence of notions respecting us which may, possibly, be entertained by men of narrow information; as little could we notice a possible suggestion that we make so plain avowals in a spirit of subservience. No one who has any just sense of our position as citizens of the United States, can suppose us to be so little mindful of our country's honor. But it merely may not be out of place to make known to our distinguished guests, and through them to the public of Melbourne that these are the feelings and sentiments with which we celebrate our first national anniversary in this important colonial town—this new Ophir of the southern seas.

We can only just recur once more to the more personal thoughts and emotions which crowd upon us in observing the "fourth" in this peculiar place and time, and which none but native-born Americans can appreciate. We think of the wide oceans which lie between us, and the kindred and friends whom distance cannot make us cease to remember; the scenes of former such days move in silent procession through our memories, and we perplex our fancies vainly to image what will be doing to-night on the other side of the orb. There are those who will think of us, as we of them; among them those who will smile to read a few months hereafter the names of us who are keeping this festival. Our hearts have not travelled. We have not forgotten what our fathers accomplished; neither has our native land ceased to seem to us the fairest on which the sun shines.

It is no ostentatious form of words, but the sentiment of every heart of hearts, that we cannot wear a worthier name, or bear a prouder title, than that we claim by birthright as citizens of the United States of North America. (Cheers.)

G. W. Peck.

Ship Albus, Melbourne, 29th June, 1853

Mr. Mowton proposed the first regular toast of the evening—"The day we celebrate." Received with three times three, with music; and when the band had ceased, he intimated that the meeting was open to any volunteer toast which any gentleman present might choose to propose. The invitation not being responded to,

Mr. Mowton gave next, "Her Most Gracious Majesty, the Queen of England." He need only say that that was a toast to which all Englishmen would heartily drink bumpers.

Received with enthusiastic cheers; air, God Save the Queen, and at its close a hearty triple hip, hip, hurrah, was given throughout the room.

Third toast.—"The President of the United States." (Cheers.) Air, Hail Columbia.

Fourth toast.—H. R. H. Prince Albert, and the royal family. Operatic air, *Suona il tromba Trepida.*

Dr. Iffla here rose and said; Mr. Chairman and gentlemen, if you will allow me, I will offer a toast; it is to the memory of the signers of that immortal document—the first in war, the first in peace—those who will ever remain embalmed in the hearts of their countrymen—the signers of the "Declaration of Independence."

Drunk in solemn silence.

Mr. Mowton: I have now to propose the fifth regular toast of the evening; and I have no doubt every gentleman present, whether English or American, or whatever nation he may happen to be, will join me in the toast. The toast, then, gentlemen, which I have the honor to propose to you is, "The memory of George Washington."

Drunk up-standing, and in solemn silence.'

Mr. Mowton: The sixth toast is—"His Excellency the Lieutenant-Governor of the Colony of Victoria," and on proposing that toast, I will read to you the reply which our chairman received to the invitation sent to His Excellency to honor the occasion we now celebrate with his presence. It is as follows:—

"GOVERNMENT OFFICES, MELBOURNE,
June 29, 1853.

"SIR,—The Lieutenant-Governor begs to acknowledge the receipt of your polite note, conveying an invitation from the American residents of the city of Melbourne, to dine with them on Monday, July 4th. His Excellency desires me to express his regret that he is precluded from accepting invitations to public dinners.

"I have the honor to be, Sir,
" Your most obedient servant,
"NORMAN CAMPBELL,
"P. Sec."

J. A. HENRIQUES, Esq.

The toast was drunk.

Mr. Throckmorton here rose to interpose a toast. He wished them to drink to one of their steam-men—the first man in that city who had ever put steam and steam machinery upon their river, and kept it there too. He proposed, then, "the health of their worthy guest Captain Cole." (Cheers.) May he live long and die happy, and go to heaven by steam, or electric telegraph. (Cheers and laughter.)

Capt. Cole acknowledged the compliment. His friend had taken him rather aback. He would try and not go out of this world quite as quick as his friend would send him. (Hear, hear.) He begged to thank them for the manner in which they had received his name. He felt proud of meeting his friends the American residents of Melbourne on the present occasion. He had met the men of the United States before; he had met them in peace and in war, and he knew how to appreciate them in both capacities. (Hear, hear.) He had great pleasure in again thanking them for the honor they had done him. He wished, old as he was, he had a little of that life and energy which the Americans possessed in advancing things and sending them forward; but he hoped that matters in the colony would go ahead better for the future than they had hitherto done. The colony of Victoria was a young country, only sixteen years old, and of these he had been thirteen years a resident in it. They had been going on quietly prosperous, from the natural resources of the country, when the unexampled treasures which must speedily make it a great and mighty country were discovered. They should endeavor to meet that discovery with a corresponding amount of energy, and then they would go a-head. The laws of their country would give every protection to those who came amongst them, let their nation be what it might. (Cheers.)

Seventh regular toast—"The Pine of Carolina—The Elm of Marshfield, and the Oak of Marshfield,—the fallen Monarchs of the American Forest, where so oft our Eagle rested,—the immortal trio of patriotic statesmen whose eloquence ornaments the nineteenth century,—may their memory be as precious as were their lives valuable to their country,—Calhoun, Clay, Webster."

Drunk up-standing, in solemn silence. Air:—Auld Lang Syne.

Mr. Steele wished to volunteer a toast, viz., "The Memory of the Great Hero of Waterloo."

Mr. Mowton begged to interpose. That was the next toast on the docket, viz., the eighth regular toast, and it was as follows:—

"To the Memory of the Great Statesman and Soldier, His Grace the Duke of Wellington, and the distinguished Champion of Free Trade, Sir Robert Peel." Music. Drunk in silence.

Ninth toast.—"The Home of our Nativity. So long as the tablets of the memory retain the impression of the past, we can never forget its hallowed associations." (Cheers.) Air—Home, sweet Home.

Mr. Mowton: Next to our own home we give The home of our Adoption. May the influence that has drawn thousands to its shores, result in permanent benefit to the Colony of Victoria." (Cheers.) Air—There's a Good Time Coming.

Mr. Dalgety responded to the toast. Although not the oldest resident of Victoria present, still he should feel himself wanting in courtesy if he showed any reluctance, when called upon, to acknowledge the toast. He had great pleasure in seeing so many American gentlemen amongst them in Melbourne. Far from entertaining any jealousy, as a merchant, on that score, he felt that the field was wide enough for them all. He was happy, then, on the present occasion, to make the acquaintance of many of those gentlemen, whom he had hitherto been unable to meet. As an old colonist, he rejoiced to see so many new faces amongst them, and he had no doubt that many of the colonists would "gain a wrinkle," from their introduction amongst them. (Cheers and laughter.)

Eleventh toast:—"La Belle France, and all civilized nations of the world."

Music.

Mr. Mowton begged to introduce the twelfth toast, as one that came from his heart, viz.—The Armies and Navies of Great Britain and America. May the harmony and good feeling which now exist between them never be interrupted; and may that day never arrive when their flags shall be unfurled in warfare with each other." (Cheers.)

Airs, Rule Britannia and Yankee Doodle.

The thirteenth and last regular toast was—"The daughters of England and America. May their bright example and virtues be beacons to guide us to prosperity and happiness." (Cheers.)

Air, Here's a health to all good lasses.

After the regular toasts came volunteer toasts, and speeches from American and English gentlemen, of the character and variety usual on such occasions, but which it would occupy too much space to include here. The above was thought to be of sufficient interest, as being the *first* Fourth of July celebrated in the province, and as exhibiting the feeling subsisting between the English and American merchants, to be inserted.

I have not thought it necessary to protract my sketch with an account of the mines and mining operations, which have been so often described in our own and the London journals. The interest in them has here somewhat declined, and enough of my own impressions will have appeared incidentally in the course of my narrative. I could not write what would attract those wishing to emigrate, or gratify my commercial friends engaged in the Australian trade; and I have so much disinclination, that I have hardly the ability to write at all upon the subject of gold mining.

THE CHINCHAS.

I.

After looking out all day, we made land on the evening of the 13th of September, just before sunset—a dim outline of mountains, barely distinguishable through the hazy loom to the eastward. Our captain judged our position to be to windward, that is to the southward of our port of destination, about forty miles, and accordingly kept away before the light wind under short sail for the night. In the morning, the island of San Lorenzo, which is the barrier that forms the roadstead of Callao, lay full in sight about twenty miles E. N. E. It is about seven miles long by one or more wide, and is a perfectly desolate ridge of volcanic rock and sand rising out of the sea twelve hundred feet in the highest part, which is towards the northern end, where it terminates in a straight steep slope, round which vessels pass to enter the roads. Being of a marked form, and the only large island for a long dis tance on the coast, it is easily recognized by all mariners who have ever once made it. On the south are two other islets or heaps of rock attending it, and other smaller ones on the seaward side, one of which, as well as one within the harbor, has a hole or arch worn through it.

The wind continued light all the morning, and it was not till afternoon that we rounded the point, and came in sight of the port of Callao with its shipping and the plain of Lima, the white line of whose churches is just visible over the green distance at the base of the mountains. As we proceeded up the bay we could hear the whistle of the locomotive that runs every two hours between the port and the city, and could distinguish the castle and a few mean-looking buildings, which are all that can be seen of the splendors of Callao from the water. We came to anchor about two o'clock, among a fleet of a hundred sail or more, Americans, (chiefly) English, French, Dutch, Peruvians, &c. Our berth was near the long narrow beach, on the other side of which the surf was breaking, and which extends out in nearly a right angle with the shore more than half way to San Lorenzo, four miles from the port.

About four o'clock we got into shore-boats, and were pulled ashore through the flocks of pelicans to the stairways inside the mole, where we disembarked, glad enough to reach the land once more; even the earthquaken sand of Callao seemed *terra firma* after the oscillations and undulations we had experienced for more than two months in a ship which, for want of ballast, appeared to be afflicted with a constant vertigo.

The first view of Callao is not imposing. You ascend the stairs, and go round the nearest corner that seems to look like a street, and come upon a mud-walled lane, full of sailors and blacks, of all shades of color, Peruvians and mules. Crossing this and proceeding up half a dozen rods, or not so much, you come to a ship-chandler's shop, (Velasquez & Lyons) all open to the street, where there are usually a group of captains sitting on old chairs, as in a Dutch grocery in Western New York. Opposite, on the right hand corner, is another similar shop and group of sitters (Bryce's.) Directly in front goes down a narrow, ill-paved, dirty-looking lane of one and a half story mud-walled buildings, occupied by clothing shops and the usual retail trumpery of the marine quarters of our cities—only the lane looks infinitely narrower and more dingy and out of repair than Ann or Cherry street. On the left hand is the "Marine Hotel," which you set down as being the meanest of sailor taverns, and afterwards discover to be the principal commercial house of the place. Nothing can be conceived more forlorn than the *tout ensemble* of Callao on a first introduction, especially to one who never saw a Spanish town. I looked at the thick mud walls, thought of the earthquakes; the accounts in the old school geographies; the yarns I had heard time out of mind from old whaling friends, all now married off, and retired in villages at home; wondered at the donkeys, the inconceivable dirt of their drivers, the gay dresses of the women, the extraordinary appearance of the soldiers, and the littleness and compactness of the whole place, which seems to be an old tumble-down seaport compressed into the smallest possible dimensions—reduced to its lowest terms. Meanwhile, as I stood on the corner, I was several times accosted as captain, in the politest manner imaginable, and was obliged finally to confess myself only a passenger to escape importunities of the kindest and most pressing character. Presently, as I started to walk up the street, my eye fell upon a familiar face—a face which instantly turned with reciprocal regard towards mine. We approached, shook hands, —an old College friend, and I, who could not remember having seen him for nearly twice ten years; he now captain of a tall ship, and I a wayfarer, but neither of us feeling a moment older than when we last met. It was odd, to say the least, that we should meet here—a coincidence, as Mr. Pickwick's friend would have remarked. We were both going to the Chinchas, where frequently afterwards we had opportunities of talking over the old times, and imparting and receiving information of the old boys; who had become lawyer, who doctor, who had gone into trade, who was married, who dead, who missionary to India—who had got in the State Prison and the like—reminiscences which all collegians in the United States know to be the most interesting subject for exchanging notes upon in the world. I mention this meeting, because it shows how singularly the skeins of these lives of ours are tangled together; and also how difficult it is for one in this year of the world to reach a spot where his dream of romance shall not be interrupted by some simple circumstance reminding him of his youth and his home.

I do not recollect whether there were any quarrels of sailors in the street while —— and myself were speaking together; if there were none during the space of half an hour, it was rather remarkable. Generally on the principal corner, there is a succession of parties of Jack-tars who are never all sober at once, and are usually discussing or making merry after their fashion when ashore. The whole place is little else but a slop-shop, model lodging house and shipping office. The men are nearly all sharks, the women all black-eyed, and black-faced Susans, the houses are mostly low mud-walled boxes with a parlor bed-room open to the street, and a kitchen back. Half the time as one passes along, he will see in the front apartment a sharp Yankee swinging in a hammock, and smoking a paper cigar, while in a rocking chair sits an Africo-Spanish woman with bright eyes and small hands, dressed in the tawdriest colors possible, but looking old enough to be his mother—so quickly does the life, or the climate, or both, of Callao fade them. Enter, and the chances are that the said Yankee inquires about Beverly, or knows your business, or has seen you somewhere else; he is, or has been mate of some vessel. Sometimes he is evidently an old hand, worthy to compete with any of our sailor-boarding house keepers in New York. At all events, you may be generally sure of civil treatment from him so long as you behave well yourself. I would recommend, however, that tourists wishing to acquaint themselves with Callao, should take no more money with them than is barely necessary; they may lose it.

All, or nearly enough all to say so, of the houses in Callao, are open to the street and to strangers; walk in, and ask to light your cigar in Spanish, the answer is, "Why not?" or walk in without ceremony, if you speak no Spanish; sit down, call for a glass of Italia, or the like; pay for it a real, make yourself agreeable, it's all right. If there is a guitar, and you can play ever so little, you will need no letter of introduction. Some of the Spanish Quadroons you will see, must be the indigenous growth of Callao; their eyes are burning coals, and in their complexions you may see the volcanic fire raging just under the skin. They look like bronze Venuses heated to redness. Traveller!

venture not alone into such temptation unless the image of an ideal lady sits enshrined in your heart!

I walked round to the castle. It is a large circular tower, enclosing a court-yard containing buildings, on the central one of which is a small steeple and the town clock, Round it is a deep and wide dry ditch made by the angular wall or embankment which surrounds the whole. The tower, and the walls, and buildings, are all of adobes, or large sun-burnt bricks, which, though soft, are probably a good defence against heavy shot when laid in walls of so great thickness. On one side of the tower, I observed many contusions which seemed to have been made by cannon shot in some of the revolutions. This castle has been the key to Peru; the parties who have held it successively have been the actual parties in power, and it is therefore, though hardly more of a fortification, at least to my inexperienced eye, than the deserted ones along our coast, a very conspicuous object in Peruvian history. It is now the barracks of a small detachment of soldiers, the police, I presume, of Callao. A gun is fired from it every night at nine o'clock.

The Peruvian soldiers are among the curiosities of the country, both in Callao and Lima. They are mostly not over five feet in height, and are round and narrow in the shoulders, and stoop as they stand in their ranks, which are anything but regular. They are very dark, and from their high cheeks, Aztec noses, and straight black hair, I supposed them to be of the native Indian blood of the country, more or less pure—descendants of the Incas. Their faces had all a family likeness, and a character of simplicity and good nature, mixed with hardness and cruelty. A company of them marching two and two, lock step, through a street, would be hissed off the stage of the Chatham, appearing as the soldiers in Don Cesar de Bazan. The officers were better, and I wondered that they were not, like Falstaff, ashamed of their soldiers. But as I observed them closely, it was evident that they too were mere men of apparel—knights of the carpet. Some that I saw in Lima had an excellent style of manner, as well as sweetly padded coats, and were really very gentlemanlike persons, but they failed to impress me with that sense of reality which I like to feel in the society of military men.

Some of the troops were mounted. I never saw such men or such horses anywhere else; and to see both in combination, was almost overpowering. The soldiers are all clad in a sort of reddish gray uniform with small caps; their suits seldom fit them, and they wear their accoutrements in the most awkward manner. On foot, they look like a chain gang dressed up; mounted, I know not what to compare them to. I could hardly realize that they were living beings—they looked more like scare-crow figures made of suits of clothes, stuffed out with straw. The infantry who officiate as the night patrol in Callao, are very kind to strangers, long-suffering and accommodating.

I several times accosted them, and walked on a little with them around the outskirts; they invariably offered to procure me an hospitable reception in some agreeable family where a single gentleman might enjoy the comforts of a home—for a very small sum in advance, pecuniary compensation being apparently less regarded in Callao than society. One evening one of them picked my handkerchief from my pocket while I was talking with him; I felt the operation, but he wore a sword, and our ship was to sail next day—and besides, the handkerchief was an ancient one and I knew that I had plenty more. I therefore set it down among the incidental expenses travellers are obliged to pay for their learning. Notwithstanding the unfavorable impression which these weaknesses of character in members of the patrol might create respecting that body, I am rather inclined to think Callao a safe enough place to well disposed Americans or Englishmen. There are always knowing ones of these two nations hovering about, and any gross wrong is pretty sure to be righted, sailor fashion. There are Germans, also, and Dutch, and in such a place, all the old sea lions make common cause; unless one strays off alone, and forgets utterly next morning where he went, and what became of his money, I apprehend there are always shipmates enough within hearing to prevent any imposition. I went everywhere—to the dance halls, and the "mascaras," and saw nothing worse than noise, and fun, and gay dresses. To a mere outside barbarian, the whole town seems to enjoy a perpetual holiday.

Generally, while the ship remained, I slept on board and spent as much time at the port and in Lima as I could. I was ashore every day I was in Lima, including both visits, nearly a week. But I kept no journal of each particular day's doings, and shall therefore present my observations collectively in the order they happen to occur to my recollection, as I am now writing, on board the good ship Tornado, in the second week from Callao, lon. 88° west, and about the latitude of Valparaiso. Every thing is fresh in my mind, and I have so much to tell that my only trouble is the *embarrass du richesse.* I was passenger in the Albus while she lay at Callao, from Sept. 14th to Sept. 23d, when I left in her for the Chincha Islands. We arrived there Oct. 3d, and I remained on board her till Nov. 10th, when I took passage on the Tornado, which was to reach New York sooner, and came back to Callao the next day. This time I had another week for observation, as we did not sail upon the present voyage home till the 19th. I think I will now leave Callao for the Chinchas, and resume Lima, (the very sound of which word affects me now like some lively, half melancholy Spanish dance,) till my return. Old sailors must be allowed to spin their yarns after their own fashion.

But before concluding this initiatory chapter, let me congratulate myself in a few words on the circumstances under which I am at this moment writing. It is a pleasant afternoon; the wind is light and nearly aft. We are heading S. half W., with studding sails set for Cape Horn. The Tornado is one of the largest and finest clippers out of New York—a ship which a few years since would have been a marvel among merchant vessels. She has on board a cargo of upwards of two thousand tons. Her main deck is 230 feet long. She has a crew of fifty men, and the accommodations of her cabin are equal in spaciousness and comfort to those of any first class frigate. We are only seven at table, including five passengers, with the Captain and first officer, so that we have "ample room and verge enough." I could even, were I disposed to that amusement, "swing a cat" in my state room. Although there is a heavy swell even now setting from the southward, the motion of the ship is so slight as scarcely to be perceptible; and I hardly realize that I am at sea, though we shall have been a fortnight out to-morrow. There have also been sea incidents; one of the men, a Swede, jumped overboard just at nightfall, Nov. 21st, and could not be found; day before yesterday, the 30th, we had a solar eclipse as predicted in the Greenwich almanac, and to-day we have been attended by our first albatross. Listen, ye who love to read of adventures in the extreme regions of what Sinbad, that renowned and veracious traveller, calls the "four seas," to the narrative of the Islands of the Sea Lions.

II.

The Chinchas are three small islands lying outside the bay of Pisco, about ninety miles down the coast, or southward from San Lorenzo, and fourteen miles from the main land. Although the distance is so small, the passage to them from Callao is usually a long and wearisome one, the trade winds blowing nearly a-head off shore, and merging into, and losing themselves in calms and land and sea breezes, generally contrary within sight of the coast. No directions can be given for beating up this passage; sometimes vessels make good runs by short stretches, keeping in shore; others do well by running out into the trades, and making all their latitude in a single tack—and vice versa in both cases. The Albus got under weigh, and made sail about two in the afternoon of Friday the 23d. We took the trades blowing fresh just outside of San Lorenzo, and our Captain judged it best to make a long leg by running well out, hoping thus to keep in the strong wind and avoid the calms and uncertain airs of the coast. Accordingly, we stood out southwestwardly till Sunday morning, when we wore ship and stood in to see how much we had made; for the weather had been too thick for an observation, and our Captain began to suspect from his reckoning, that we were not doing so well as he had hoped. The ship was in no condition to beat up to windward on account of her light ballast. The old crew who had brought her from Port Phillip, having shipped only for the run, had been discharged at Callao, and a new crew shipped, consisting of Cholos, or the mixed blood of the Indian and white, especially for service at the Islands. These had been shipped by the Captain of the Port, who is in fact only a shipping master, and whose representations are said not to be so perfectly reliable as might be desired. In the present case the poor Cholos, most of whom could understand but little English, had been made to believe that they only shipped to take in guano; only two or three of them were ordinary seamen; the rest were "boys" and they were all smaller and of less strength and lighter weight than so many Lascars. They were not strong enough to work the ship, even had they been sailors. Our Captain had, therefore, good reason for deeming it imprudent to venture out further into the strong winds, where we could only carry reefed top sails, with such a crew.

Monday morning, the 26th, we were all on the lookout for land again, expecting to have made a third of our passage at least. But lo and behold, when we at last succeeded in making it out through the haze that always hovers over these arid coasts in the early part of the day, what should it be but our old acquaintance San Lorenzo! We had been three days out, and our poor Cholos had performed miracles in the way of shortening sail, and the rest of us, the Captain, a fellow-passenger, and myself, had held on for three mortal days like so many patiences at sea, to find we had hardly made three miles of our course. Nothing is so disheartening to landsmen as the disappointments and delays of beating dead to windward. This occasion the Captain used afterwards to aver was the only time the courage of his two passengers failed them; we said nothing, but if he had offered us the "Pet," (the ship's gig,) I have no doubt we should have gladly taken her and pulled back to Callao, which lay in sight, and left him to work up to the Chinchas alone.

But captains are a most persevering as well as an imperative race; we knew we were in for it, and had no more to do but to make the best of it. We now, instead of standing far out, made short tacks, three and four in a day, generally reaching out in the latter part of the night and running into catch the land breeze in the morning. But it was slow work; the captain took the wheel, and we passengers assisted in tacking and wearing. I believe we were a whole week in sight of our old friend San Lorenzo, and I have in my mind as perfect a chart of that part of the Peruvian coast, as I have of the coast of New York from Sandy Hook to New York, or of Boston Bay, or the Narragansett.

I recollect, one fine afternoon when we were sailing leisurely and calmly under a slight breeze, ten or fifteen miles from the shore, F—— called me from the cabin to look at what he said were the Andes. When I came on deck he pointed to a blue outline away up in the sky, at least a sixth part, or fifteen degrees of the way from the horizon to the zenith. We had previously seen what we had been admiring as lofty mountains in the immediate vicinity of Lima, and along the coast. The range runs higher than any land in the United States. But the present blue outline was so immeasurably above them that I could not at first bring myself to believe it to be the outline of mountains, and we had quite an argument. But I was forced to yield. The forms did not change. With the glass we could see what must be mighty rocks upon their summits, and could distinguish the ravines and ridges on their sides. I shall never forget or be able to describe the effect of the first view of them. As the sun fell they became lighted up, and the whole side of the range was of a dull yellow; we knew that it must be the reflection of the sun upon the glaciers, but it looked like yellow sand. Indeed the forms of the mountains at the distance which we saw them from, nearly ninety miles, as we afterwards ascertained, appeared precisely like so many ridges of gravel heaped up and worn into ravines and ridges by rains—like what we may see on the sides of high railroad embankments. But the immense height—the perfect stillness—I cannot tell how awful and at the same time how glorious it is. These same ridges we saw every clear afternoon while we lay at the Chinchas, forty miles further South, so little did that distance change their angle. I was never tired of looking at them, and I always felt by night and day that they were looking down upon us and watching the great ocean. At the Chinchas it is about sixty miles from the shore to their bases, and when their summits are reached, those who have crossed their passes have described to me how others appear still higher, and whose tops are always lost in clouds. We were told that the highest part of the Andes range was now believed to lie in this latitude.

What a beautiful world this is! But for some old simple necessities and wishes, I could live anywhere upon it forever; and as it is, I fancy it would take more than an ordinary lifetime to tire one of life in this enchanted region. But then I love music and the society of ladies and old friends. I shall not return to, and end my days in, some valley of the Andes until they have all died off—my mother, whom I could not live without, and all the rest. So much for my ideas of life; we must have a little individuality in a book or it is not worth much, to my thinking.

SUNDAY, OCT. 2.—We had a favorable wind for our landward tack in the afternoon, and at nightfall as it died away, we were becalmed within a few miles of the Chinchas and in sight of the shipping. Compared with the coast we had passed, and with the highlands of Paraca Point and San Gallan Island, which lies ten miles or more to the southward, they look from a distance like some insignificant rocky islets covered with yellow sand. But as we approach and count the ships that lie in under their lee, their real height becomes more apparent.

Early Monday morning we had a visit from Capt. H—— of the Duchess d'Orleans, (a name not unfamiliar to New York ears,) who came out to pilot us to a berth in the fleet. This was in conformity to the custom established here among the Captains, and by which every ship that arrives is visited and brought into her anchorage by some of those whose vessels are waiting their turn for a cargo, and who know the ground—a convenient as well as hospitable mode of welcome, which saves much care and trouble to shipmasters visiting the islands for the first time. A little distinction is made in this and other customs of the islands, respecting launches and the like, among the English and American captains, but there is not much; each feels more particularly called to render assistance to ships of his own nation, " but all is kindly done," and all give and expect the same cordial reception on the decks of each vessel. In all these things the courtesy of the sea has its laws as well as that of the land; and when there are so many captains assembled at the Chinchas, and kept so long waiting through needless delays, the unsocial and disagreeable characters, it may be supposed, have not the advantage of any pecular facilities in despatching their business.

At breakfast time we were still in all but a dead calm, about three miles to the northward of the North Island, outside of the ships, more than half of which are anchored there. There is very seldom a breeze from the north, and never a strong one, so that this is the lee side on both the north and the middle islands. Here vessels and launches are loaded; many ships moor close in to the precipice of rocks with their stern in and bows out, but most are anchored at various distances within half or three quarters of a mile. There was usually about sixty vessels anchored and moored at the North island, and as many more at the middle. I sent a list home to the New York *Times*, containing one hundred and fourteen, but it was necessarily incomplete, owing to the constant arrivals and departures.

The wind continuing light, we did not make much progress all the early part of the forenoon. Our ship was to lie at the Middle island, and to do this it was necessary to pass the North one and make a stretch up the bay. As we did this and came round, about eleven o'clock, to run in for the middle anchorage, several boats came off with other captains; and Cape Cod, and Connecticut, and New York, and down East generally, shook hands with Marblehead; Cape Cod, if I remember rightly, took the wheel, and New York continued to act as pilot till they ran the ship in among the others, about midway between the eastern ends of the Middle and North islands, where she let go her anchor about one o'clock.

By that time the breeze had freshened, and blew right off the point of the Middle island, laden with the dust and odor of guano. This breeze blows regularly every day, and is called the "Paraca," because it blows from Paraca Point, I suppose; it usually sets in about one or two o'clock, but sometimes begins earlier,as it did the morning we came in. Towards evening it often blows a strong breeze, and gets up a surf on the weather side of the islands from the southeast in the course of an hour or two, that makes it difficult for boats to land there. We anchored in about thirty fathoms water; vessels, by the way, are very apt in coming in here not to have sufficient chain overhauled for such a depth of water, and are liable to drift from their position before the anchor bites, and in consequence, to run afoul of other vessels, where they all lie as near to each other as they can with safety. All ships should have at least fifty fathoms of chain ready to run clear.

I did not go ashore till the next morning after my arrival, when ——, whom I mentioned having met at Callao, took me with him to the Middle island. The landing is under the precipice, on a ledge that makes out in front of a great cave, extending quite through the point, over which, a hundred feet above, project shears for hoisting up water and provision. On the ledge, a staircase, or rather several staircases, go up in a zigzag to close by the foot of the shears; the lowest staircase, about twenty feet long, hangs from shears at the side of the ledge at right angles with the rest in front of the cave, and is rigged to be hoisted or lowered according to the tide, and to be drawn up every evening, or whenever the Governor of the Island chooses to enjoy his dignity alone.

A few rods from the edge of the cliff, directly over the cave, is the palace of the said governor, who styles himself in all his State papers,

"KOSSUTH."

The palace is a large flat-roofed shanty, constructed of rough boards and the canes and coarse rush matting which answers generally for the commonest sort of dwellings in Peru. It has, if I remember correctly, two apartments, with a sort of portico, two or three benches, a table and grass hammock in front surrounded by a low paling, forming a little yard, where a big dog usually mounts guard. One of the apartments is probably the store-room; there is a kitchen shanty adjoining the piazza on the side most exposed to the sun. The other is the bed-chamber and dining-room of Governor Kossuth and his aids. It contains three or four cot beds, an old table and writing desk, and is decorated with a few newspapers, colored lithographs, and old German plans of the battles of Frederick the Great. Over Kossuth's couch are some cheap single barrel pistols; the floor is guano. The situation overlooks nearly all the shipping between the Middle and North islands. Directly under it, but far beneath, the cavern from before which the stairs go up, runs through and opens into a narrow bight or cove, whose precipices reach up to within a few yards of the rear of the shanty. The noise of the surf comes up here in a softened monotone; below are a hundred tall vessels—the North island with its strange rocks and dark arches fringed with foam—in the distance, north and east, the hazy bay of Pisco lying in the sunshine, and if it be afternoon, the snowy Andes.

We found Kossuth at home. He is a Hungarian, or at least looks like one, and has selected a Hungarian name. He is a middle sized, half soldier-like, youngish individual, with quick gray eyes, and an overgrown red moustache.

He wears his hair trimmed close at the back of his head, which goes up in a straight wall, broadening as it goes, and causing his ears to stand out almost at right angles. From this peculiarity, as well as his general cast of countenance, he looks combative and hard. But his forehead, gathering down in a line with his nose, and his speech and actions show so much energy of character, that he does not look like a very bad fellow after all. He is full of life, and display, and shrewdness, and swearing, and broken English. I rather liked him.* His favorite exclamation is " Hellanfire !" and he loves to show his authority. He was polite enough to me, though the captains often complained of being annoyed by his caprices.

He invited me to come ashore and see him, and offered to tell me " all the secrets of the island." He told me that he was one of the party of Hungarians who came to New York on the representations of Ujhazy, who had obtained for them a grant of land. But he said, that land was of no use to them, they were soldiers—they could not work. Ujhazy, who had been a landowner at home, and not a military man, had made a blunder in obtaining land—they wanted employment in the army, or as engineers and the like. That he, (Kossuth,) finding how matters stood, left

* He appreciates Shakespeare. I gave the Spanish doctor an old copy, and Kossuth bought it of him. I told him it showed he must have some claim to his name.

New York for New Orleans, where he joined the Lopez expedition. From this he escaped, he did not tell me how, into Mexico; thence reached San Francisco, where he joined Flores, and so came to South America. Here, when that expedition failed, he took service in Peru, and finally had obtained the place he held on this island, where he said he meant to make money enough to buy land, and tell other people to work, but not to work himself. He pitied the poor Chinese slaves here, but what could he do? He could only make them work—and so on.

He talked and exclaimed "Hellanfire!" and gesticulated, altogether with so much rapidity that it was an effort to follow him; treated us to some of the wine of the country, (very much like the new wine of Sicily,) and other good things; cold ham, sardines, and preserved meats, which he says the captains present him with, more than he wants, and he never knows where they come from. According to him they all expect cargoes at once, and as he cannot accommodate them, they try to influence him by arguments and long talks and flattery, and in every sort of way, and he gets wearied to death in his efforts to please them—poor man! He told all this with a lamentable voice and face, and every now and then a roguish twinkle of the eye, that made it a great trial of the nerves to listen to him without laughing—knowing as I did the exact sum which had been paid him by some captains, to get loaded before the expiration of their lay days!

After finishing our call upon him, we walked over the height of the island; that is, over the rounded hill of guano which covers it, and of which but a small portion comparatively has been cut away on one side for shipment. The average height of the rock which is the substratum of the island, is from an hundred and fifty to two and three hundred feet. Kossuth's place stands on the surface of this at about the lowest of those elevations. On this the guano lies as upon a scaffolding or raised platform rising out of the sea. It lies on a smooth rounded mound, and is on this island about a hundred and sixty feet in the central part, supposing the rock to maintain the average level of the height when it is exposed. Perhaps twenty acres or more have been cut away from the side of the hill towards the north or lee side the island, next the shipping.

As we walked along the edge of the cove behind and within a few rods of Kossuth's house, we saw the Chinese coolies digging and wheeling, and their taskmasters looking on. A little back were the miserable cane huts where they sleep, and not far from this, within a couple of rods of where they were digging on this side, we were shocked by coming upon the dead body of one lying almost naked in the sun, with the face of it covered with flies. It was one, we afterwards ascertained, who had been drowned that morning, whether accidentally or not, nobody knew—or cared. It lay among a number of little heaps or graves, and the turkey buzzards wheeled around it almost in our faces.

Over the back of the hill we came among the little birds who swarm over the islands, wherever they are not disturbed, in multitudes which no man can number. Yet I cannot suppose that they are the principal producers of the guano, though I have repeatedly seen the surface blue with them for a space of more than ten acres; and the precipices are alive with them. The name for the species in common Peruvian, is "Poto-Huenco." They are beautiful birds, much like blue pigeons, but more lightly formed, and with fire-red bills. On each side of their heads is a single narrow yellow feather, shaped like an S, reaching half-way down their necks—an ornament conceived by Nature in one of her happiest inspirations.

When we came among these birds, they would rise in front about a rod from us, and close in behind, as we proceeded, so that we were constantly in their midst. A stick thrown among them would frighten them only for a moment; the cloud would soon settle around us again. They are so strong of wing that they fly with a peculiarly flitting airy motion, like so many sheets of paper blown by the wind, and they have only one plaintive note, of a quality like the human voice, and a melancholy unearthly effect that I cannot describe. In the midst of one of their great assemblies, a visiter is evidently an object of extreme curiosity; all eyes are upon him; thousands of the more venturous are flitting all about him, and apparently inquiring what sent him into their domains, and warning him to go away. "Wah, wah," they say, "what do you here? Leave this place—leave this place. It is wild and sad—wah, wah. It is ours; leave it. Fly away—away. Wah, wah, wah!" They always made me feel as if I had wandered into a congregation of ghosts or elemental spirits.

Besides these blue ones, there is a species of white ones also very numerous. They are a little larger than the blue, and snow-white. What has a very singular effect when they are all sitting together, covering acres of the sloping hills of guano, the white keep by themselves in the midst of the blue, like the staff of a great army, or like a division of allies in different uniform. The white ones also abound on the precipices, where I believe both they and the blue have their nests. Besides these, there are beautiful little black-winged, white-breasted birds, not larger than squab pigeons, who have their nests in holes in the guano, about a foot beneath the surface, and three feet within. The guano is everywhere perforated and honeycombed with these holes, and the birds may be taken from them any time by reaching in the hand. One day when we went gunning, two men took out more than fifty in a short time. I carried one to the ship and kept him a day or two, intending to preserve him, but my heart relented. I had suffered on account of my cape pigeon. I bethought me that not being a naturalist, the good of science did not require me to stuff birds, and so I let him go over the gunwale. The moment he touched the water he was out of sight.

All these birds, and many more that abound on the islands, are birds of the sea. The white may be seen off the coast of Peru many miles from land. The blue are constantly fishing around the islands; wherever there is a school of smelt or other small fish, there will be hundreds of them hovering above, diving and splashing.

Besides the birds, the only living thing upon the islands is a species of lizard from three to ten inches long, very active, and very glad to get out of the way. It is quite harmless, but will glide on a few steps aside, and turn and puff out its chin like a frog, and make a low faint croak, and presto! if you lift a stick or start, it vanishes into the next hole, and another one pops out somewhere else.

The lookout from either of the islands is enchanting. Imagine the Andes and the Pacific in one view—the islands with their precipitous walls indented with immense caves, and surrounded by fantastic rocks, fringed with foam—the pure ocean air—the myriads of sea birds—the shipping—the schools of sea lions—and almost always, far or near upon the blue waste—the spout of whales, and the white sails of ships coming or departing—altogether the scene is full of exhilaration and excitement. The height of the islands is such, that the eye looks directly down upon the masts of the vessels moored and lying beneath, and the round horizon demonstrates to the eye the appropriateness of the phrase of the Admiralty Courts, "the high seas."

The Middle island is a little longer east and west than the north, but its superficial extent must be about the same. Neither of them are more than a mile across in the widest part. The south island is somewhat smaller, but is quite as high. It has not yet been dug from, probably on account of the greater exposure to the surf, and consequent difficulty of loading launches.

The guano where exposed to the air, is of a reddish brown, yellow color, darker than that of its general substance, where it is cut away. It of course colors the whole of the islands, the rock on which it rests being only visible round the shores. As it is like light dry earth, and full of holes, it is difficult to walk upon, there being no certainty that every other footstep will not sink in nearly to the knee. If one hurries he is almost sure to fall, or rather to get into it all over, in which case the only satisfaction is in knowing that it is almost pure ammonia, and contains no animal substance, otherwise it might be thought to be an unpleasant sticky sort of soil. A few feet below the surface it becomes compact, and from thence through its whole thickness is of nearly the consistence of Castile soap. Its odor is strongly ammonical, though this is not perceived, or but faintly, in walking over the islands where they have not been dug upon.

We went upon the edge of the cutting, where the Chinese coolies or slaves, who are the only laborers here, are employed daily in cutting away the hill with pickaxes, and conveying the guano to the edge of the cliff in barrows. From the shipping the cutting appears almost perpendicular, and the slaves are just visible here and there on the side like so many insects. But from the top it is seen to slope at a convenient angle for pushing down the guano as fast as it is picked away and broken up to be loaded into the barrows at the base. There are about three hundred coolies on the middle island, and from seven to eight hundred on the north. They are kept at work by black drivers—hideous creatures, who walk among them with heavy thongs; they are half naked, and their wild looks and strange cries, with the knowledge of their hard fate, make the scene of their labor a horrid place to look down upon, both at first and ever after. I shall defer to speak of their condition however, until after describing the islands more particularly.

I returned to the ship in time to dine. We had an excellent dinner, I remember, fresh beef from Pisco, which lies in the bight of the bay to which it gives its name, and is the principal town or port on this part of the coast. There was also a bushel basket of fruit at hand to draw upon next morning, which I hold to be the proper time for eating fruit—oranges, bananas, papinos, cherimoyas, paltas, and such like varieties. The oranges are the sweetest I ever tasted. I will not record how many some of us acquired the art of flaying at a sitting. The papinos are little cantelope-flavored melons, with a smooth rind; when fully ripe, the whole substance of them dissolves in the mouth. But the cherimoyas! shut your eyes and fancy yourself eating strawberries and cream—the illusion will be perfect. The very look of them, with their bulbous shape about the size of a fist, and dark green chequered rind, has a tropical flavor. Their only fault is their excess of perfection; one cannot devour a bushel of them. The paltas, or huge pears with a round stone, were the only novelty I could not admire. Most persons relish them exceedingly; to me they were so many green squashes.

III.

The Chinchas are composed of a dull whitish, and reddish colored rock, which I presume to be chiefly fieldspar or porphyry. The rock exhibits in its structure a partial stratification or crystallization in lines at angles of about twenty degrees with the horizon towards the ocean, and sixty or seventy degrees *from* it. The detached rocks, many of them very large and of the most fantastic forms conceivable, appear to have been broken from the general mass. Occasionally, but not frequently, there occur veins of trap. The whole appears to have been formed by separate inundations of lava under great pressure, probably at the bottom of the ocean. Both the character of the rock, and the contour of its surface, favor such an hypothesis. The rock has the look of a cinder produced on a great scale, and its surface appears never to have supported any other rock, but to have cooled in an uneven bubbly mass, just as it might be imagined lava would cool under such circumstances. It is full of irregular smooth elevations, and depressions, as if it had gradually subsided when viscous from a state of ebullition; and it reminded me every time I looked at it, to compare it to the structure of an old-fashioned tough-crusted apple pie. There have apparently several layers of lava contributed to its formation; as each cooled, vapors, or expansive agencies within, forced up the crust in tumid swellings, that became indurated in that shape, and were filled in beneath by rock, which by cooling as it flowed in, was less crystallized and of softer quality. This, by the action of the sea, has worn away, and produced the caves and hollow arches which are the greatest curiosity of the islands, and have perfectly adapted them to become the home of seals and birds.

The precipices around each of the islands and of the Ballista group, which is of similar formation, ten miles to the southward, are entirely perforated with immense caves that often leave only a thin crust above them, and extend in no one can tell how far, since only a few of them can be ventured into on account of the surf that rolls in great waves into them, with thundering noises and perpetual turmoil. Far within, the dark dripping ledges may be seen covered with nests and birds wherever nests can be stuck or birds stand, and along with the wind and spray that rushes out as the waves advance, come the hoarse cries of penguins and sometimes the roar of sea lions, who have their favorite haunts in such unapproachable recesses. In many instances, as under Kossuth's palace, these caves extend quite through projecting points of the island; in others, they may be plainly seen to follow far inward the contour of the swelling bubbles, as I would call them, upon the upper surface. Sometimes the rock is a hundred or two hundred feet thick over them; at others, it is a mere shell, precisely like a section of a bubble in a cinder; in a few instances is a double row more or less perfectly developed —a second story of caverns, one over the other. I speak of them as bubbles; many of them are sixty feet to their roofs, and more than that distance across. They open into each other, and in many places where boats can go in and where I have repeatedly rowed, the whole rock is a roof of immense dark domes and pillared arches, opening out in many places to the sunlight. I think I shall dream of some of these scenes hereafter.

Perhaps some of the finest of such scenery is to be found at the Ballistas which is a group much resembling the Chinchas, but higher and more exposed, and therefore affording less guano, and almost inaccessible—the only landing being upon beaches that lie at the foot of perpendicular precipices or on the points of rocks that can scarcely be climbed. We made up a party one morning and were pulled down to them by a boat's crew. We rowed through one arch on the most northerly of them a hundred feet through, but so narrow that the men were obliged to ship their oars. Though it was a calmer morning than usual, the wave sucked us in and out as easily as if the boat had been a shingle, and we had much difficulty in keeping her off the sharp points of rock on the sides. We got safely through, but none of us would have desired to risk a similar passage again, especially unless we were better acquainted with the waters beyond it; for when we got through we were nearly upon some sunken rocks almost awash in the valley of the swell. Not finding any landing place on that island, but a beach about a quarter of a mile long, which the precipice overhung, so that it would be impossible to climb to the upper regions, we pulled away for the middle island. Here we saw a beach in a small cove at the mouth of a great cave, where the sea did not appear to reach, and accordingly we made for it. As we came within the cove or bight in the precipice, for it was not more than a hundred yards across, and the rock was from a hundred and fifty to two hundred feet high, we saw that what we had taken for a cave was an immense arch, across which, about midway, the beach extended in a narrow arm. We ran the boat on this, and smooth as it appeared a little outside, we had enough to do to back her. Everything was on so large a scale that what seemed gravel was large pebbles we could hardly stand amongst, and the surf was quite sufficient to have rolled the boat over and over had we not been quick to haul her up. As it was, she filled and our lunch suffered.

But what a place we were in! Overhead was a perfectly smooth arch of rock sixty or seventy feet high, and of a hundred and fifty span, extending more than two hundred yards quite through the island. The beach we stood on formed a bar, over which, it appeared, the surf often broke, running across the eastern opening on the side we had entered, and exposed on either side to the surf. On this beach were two complete skeletons of sea lions, one with most of the skin still upon it, several skeletons of pelicans, and other scattered bones and coarse marine plants in heaps. The roar of the surf when the wave came in was so great, we could hardly distinguish what we said; it seemed to me like the voice of ages—the solemn revealing voice of Nature sounding on and on for ever. Century after century it has sounded there, and the beautiful days have glided away in this changeless climate, and all has passed in utter solitude. If I fail in expression in attempting to convey how the scene affected me, it is because I cannot yet analyze my own impressions or distinguish the threads of reverie that weave themselves about me when I think of it. All thoughts mingle together, and as I shut my eyes and call up that glorious arch and the sunshine falling against the inaccessible cliffs, and the vast ancient ocean that cannot be at rest, I become almost painfully conscious of all the circumstances of existence.

The huge skeletons of sea lions that lay upon the coarse pebbles above the reach of the surf, with the ghastly look of their skulls, were in admirable keeping with the desolation and solitude of the place. Our figures looked so small, that we seemed to have dwindled to pigmies. Our shouts rang loudly, and the report of our guns reverberated through the cool air with an echo almost deafening. Many birds were brought down from the cliffs, among them some of the blue and the white ones described in the preceding chapter, and red billed and black ducks, or birds resembling ducks, of which every rock and cliff around the islands holds a populous colony. We knocked out the canine teeth of the sea lions; they were very white and hard, three and four inches long, and curved and shaped like walrus' teeth. Underneath the cliff, on one side of the arch, were some holes or clefts in the rock on a level with the beach, within which we could just see two large birds sitting on their nests. Two or three of our keenest sportsmen set to work, and after half an hour's labor, crawling on their hands and knees, succeeded in drawing out with boathooks, two penguins, which we looked upon as the principal trophy of the expedition. They were quite indignant at the rough treatment they had received, and did not yield without obstinate resistance, one of his captors had a finger bitten to the bone. They were so strong, that one of them with one of his legs made fast by a seizing, partly unwound from an oar, would drag the oar towards the water. Every now and then they made a sound something like the lowing of a cow.

The species of penguin which frequents these islands, is from two and a half to three feet high, very dark gray on the back, with a snow white breast and two white streaks running from the eyes down each side of the neck, black bill and black flippers or fin-like wings. The usual engravings of them represent them very correctly. But they look very droll when they are alive walking on a level beach. The Peruvians call them "munos" or "baby-birds;" and in fact they look for all the world at a distance like so many children in white aprons. They step with their feet wide apart, and walk with what seems to be a ludicrous affectation of carefulness. When they get near enough they tumble, or roll, or jump, in the clumsiest manner into the water, and—disappear, to rise with just their heads out a hundred yards off. I stood upon a cliff at the Ballista, which overlooked a place below, where the sun struck into the water, and I could see the bottom where it was twenty feet under. There were many penguins diving from a rock and swimming about under water at their leisure, along with other diving birds—the ducks, before mentioned. The penguins used their flippers outspread, like seals, which they much resemble when swimming; they change their course at will, and do not hurry themselves to come to the surface. All the other divers use their feet only, and go in straight rapid lines, as if they were in haste to return to the air. The two we caught were kept alive several days on the ship. One of them was quite a match for Kangaroo, our half native Australian dog. He ultimately became a "specimen," and will probably adorn ——'s private collection. The other was made a present of, through an excess of sea politeness, to an English Captain, lying near by, who had made himself disliked on account of his surly manners. He was unacquainted with the habits and capabilities of penguins, and our worthy captain fancied that with a live one promenading his deck, he might "stand a chance" to learn something—especially if he should come within reach of his bill.

It is curious that among all the surf-beaten rocks around the islands, most of which are covered at all times with birds, the penguins select a few for their own property and allow no other species to come upon them. There they stand, looking as innocent, or rather as "cunning" (using the word in the sense we use it in speaking of children) as can be. One would never suspect them of swallowing a whole mackerel at a gulp, to watch them walking quaintly about conversing with each other, and now and then tumbling into the surf in the most awkward and undecided manner, as if they were perfectly indifferent what became of themselves. Their voices when they are swimming are very loud and deep, and somewhat resemble human cries. We heard them about the ship off the west coast of Patagonia when it was blowing heavy nearly a hundred miles from land.

We remained on the beach that ran across the arch and around the narrow cave till noon. By that time the surf had somewhat increased and it was judged best to send the boat round a point of the island and embark on the other side of the arch, where the waves were longer and the intervals between the rolls greater and more regular. We had to watch our chance to wade in and cling to the bows one or two at a time, even then. Several times the boat was near being swamped before we could succeed, and I believe all of us were quite satisfied to get aboard with only a half ducking; if some of our crew had not had experience in beach-combing, we might not have got through the surf so safely. At one time the boat turned almost end over end, and I can assure the reader that it was not pleasant to be jammed in amidships when she stood on the comb of the wave.

We pulled round towards the leeward side of the island where we had at first arrived. Not far from the great arch on the windward side of the point, round which the men had taken the boat, we pulled into the entrance of an immense dark cavern, whose roof reached so near the surface of the island, that the rock immediately overhead came out to a thin edge. It extended a hundred yards or more to the right, where there was another opening, and about the same distance on the left where were several smaller openings; but nearly in front, a little to the left, the main drift of it extended inward, preserving its height as far as we could see, into utter darkness. The mouth where we pulled in, was open to the Pacific, and it was so wide that we could lay in the middle under the roof, notwithstanding the swell. We pulled in as far as we dared, and lay cautiously on our oars watching the heave of the wave lest it should dash us upon the rocks. The fury of the sea was awful. We went in so far that we could just see immediately around us, but we could hear the roar and occasionally catch faint gleams of white foam far within. The whole cavern was perfectly alive with sea-fowl of the species of red-billed ducks or divers, before mentioned; no jutty, or projecting angle of the ledges from the roof to the edge of the foam but what had its occupant, and they were flying everywhere. Standing with their long necks stretched straight up, and perfectly still, they looked like so many imps of the infernal regions. The cavern within, must have been a hundred feet high, and not less than that in width; it is almost impossible to judge correctly where everything was so strange and so vast.

After leaving the cave we kept on to the extremity of the point, and at last found a place where we could land

and climb up to the top of the island. The rock was completely yellow, with evidence of the recent presence of birds; in the central and less exposed parts, this merged into guano, which overlays nearly the whole surface for more than a hundred acres. There were the blue birds as I had seen them on the Middle Chincha, and on the extreme points and ledges, thousand of pelicans. While my companions were shooting the blue birds by hundreds, merely for the pleasure of killing them, I went up to the south-west, or windward end, where the island terminates in cliffs three hundred feet high. I walked over the great arch and cave where we had been; on a high point I looked down upon another arch, much more elevated. It was at least a hundred and fifty feet high and two hundred across; the rock was narrow, not more than proportionably wide for such a height, to make the whole resemble a stupendous triumphal arch or gateway. A white sand-beach ran across, and the sunlight fell there so soft, and fresh, and cool, it was enough to waken one's heart to gaze upon it. I seemed to have emerged from the domains of Chaos and old Night, into a region of fairy land—such an island as young gentlemen and ladies sing duets about, intimating a mutual wish to "dwell there with thee" in the "sunny sea." Or not to degrade such matchless scenery, it gave to me the feeling of sea views in the ancient poets, in Spenser, the Tempest, the landscapes and backgrounds of the old masters, and not least, though last in the sea music of

Mendelssohn. I think if one could land within that open arch at the time of the full moon, and should see no mermaids or nymphs of the ocean there, he ought to be convinced that there are no such beings in the world.

Along in the afternoon the sky over the islands began to be filled with immense flocks of pelicans, apparently going to and from the ocean. There were even more of them than were usually seen at the Chinchas, and they flew higher, and in long lines and circles, as if they had ascended for long passages. It is not easy for those who have never visited such a coast to form an idea of the number of these and other sea birds that people this part of the ocean. For two days before we came in sight of San Lorenzo on the voyage from Australia, we sailed through myriads and myriads of them—legions innumerable, inconceivable; the green discolored sea was populous with them over all its surface as far as we could see. It was, we fancied, one of their harvest seasons, for the fish appeared to be as numerous as the birds; mackerel and herring, or fish resembling them, were constantly leaping under our bow, and the birds in some places were assembled over the shoals beneath in such numbers, that they looked like low islands as they rose on the curves of the slowly heaving undulations.

Among them were large flocks of these pelicans, a bird which is at home in almost all tropical climates, and particularly at the Chinchas, where the "Pelican war" bids fair to become hardly less celebrated than the Punic wars of ancient history. Faded, emaciated specimens of these birds, with soiled and ruffled plumage, are frequently to be seen in our travelling menageries, where their long bills and grave looks always command attention. In their native haunts, and when engaged about their ordinary avocations, their ways and doings are too remarkable not to attract much notice. On the coast of Peru, the shooting of them is a finable offence, as they are supposed to be, and it is likely are, with the seals, the principal manufacturers of what in process of time becomes guano.

In the harbor of Callao there are immense numbers of them fishing among the shipping, and from being never molested they are not in the least shy of being observed. They are very large birds, and can consume more fish in a day than several men. In this, and in consequent respects, it is not easy to over estimate their capabilities. More than a good sized bucket full of newly-caught fish have been taken from the crop of one of them! They fly heavily; the feathers at the ends of their broad wings are worn to the quill from continually beating the air and water; yet they fly long, at great heights, as well as skimming the surface, and with great power and command of their course and position. When they dive for fish, they invariably turn a back summerset and plunge down with a force and velocity quite astonishing. Their pouched bills are more than two feet long, and as they frequently rise with them apparently well filled, it is not unreasonable to conjecture that in the capacity for swallowing they are not inferior to those who believe that departed spirits can be "rapt into other times." Indeed, when they are seen standing in solemn conclaveon the rocks, they very much resemble what we should imagine to be the appearance of a convention of "spiritual rappers." I could never see them without thinking of a tea-party of venerable ladies in terested in the various benevolent "causes" of the day. Their bills are so heavy that they rest them on their necks, never extending their necks but when they dive; and they stand firm and immovable—the very impersonation of starched prudery! One lady (for there were ladies at the Chinchas,) had named them after an ancient maiden in her native village, who would doubtless, could she ever know it and see her namesakes, feel highly complimented.

In returning from our Ballista expedition we came along by the islands and caves we had passed in the morning. The sun was setting and there were splendid effects of light and shadow on the cliffs and crags. Little wind was stirring, just a light "paraca" from the South east, but the swell from the ocean had gradually increased during the day, and the surf was now tremendous on the rocks and within the immense hollows of the caverns. In the morning we had come on the windward side of the Middle and South Chinchas, where the ocean is for ever heaving and receding with a slow mighty motion, as if it were the breathing of the world. Here the rocks are whiter and the cliffs higher and more weather-worn. I know not if it is ever so calm on this side that the caves which may be seen to extend in hundreds of feet, can be ventured into with safety. The set of the great ocean waves, is so irresistible, that if a boat should once be caught by it in a narrow passage, where the whole water moves with the heave, she would be swamped in a moment. An English captain was said to have gone in his boat into one of the largest of the leeward caves, and was never seen or heard of again. But wherever the water is smooth, and only rises and descends with the wave, boats may venture; and they will go with perfect safety where to an inexperienced eye it would seem that they could not live a moment. The great height of the wave only is seen from a distance, but not its gradual slopes. On several occasions afterwards, when we had a boat's crew that could be depended on, we lay in on our oars, and even landed, and took off some of the Cholos who climbed the precipices after eggs like so many monkeys. They obtained a great many, and we had omelettes made of them, which were excellent; in boiling or frying them, the white remains trasparent.

The rocks and caverns of these islands remind me somewhat of the Pictured Rocks of Lake Superior, which I saw several years ago; I only sailed along by those, however, and did not go close in. But these volcanic rocks are much more rough and singular than the sand-stone of the Pictured Rocks, and then there is the swell of the Pacific, which on this coast is probably grander than any in any part of the world. The whole force of the trades has been expended upon the waves that prostrate themselves at the feet of the Andes. They appear the more gigantic from the constant pleasantness of the weather.

Rain, except a heavy morning mist, that sometimes leaves a few drops upon a ship's deck, is unknown; day follows day with only just change enough for variety; the mornings are generally veiled; this clears up to a sunny forenoon haze; in the afternoon comes the paracca, and the evenings are usually clear—very frequently cloudless, and with a starry sky that only the southern and middle Pacific can match for brilliance. Often when the mornings are still, and the surface of the sea undisturbed by a ripple, the surf will be rolling tremendously on the narrow beaches, and dashing in great white sheets fifty feet high or more against the precipices. These are called "surf-days," and special allowance is made for them in the charter parties of vessels loading at the islands. On such days, Governor Kossuth's stairway has sometimes to be drawn up, and it is not easy to land upon either island. As nothing can then be done on shipboard, the business of "taking in" being interrupted, it is on these days that boats go about most from ship to ship, or among the islands; for the swell is scarcely felt among the shipping, except by those vessels which are moored close in. Landsmen, and even those who may have been accustomed to the ocean as it is usually seen from our coasts, have no idea of a swell upon so large a scale. The waves are longer, and slower, and mightier; going about the shores in a boat, it would almost seem as if the very level of the sea had changed for a square mile around. At times we would be on a smooth elevation at no great distance from some inconsiderable rocks; then perhaps half a minute after, we would find ourselves in a gently curving valley, with some huge weed-covered crags an acre over, rather too near; and then would come the long rise which would seem to lift us upon them, along with an irresistible torrent.

The surf was particularly fine around the outside of the North Island. There was a passage here, called the "bucceroon passage," which boats could not always go through, and which the more venturesome were therefore always inclined to attempt. More than once in going through this, have prudent men, like myself, wished themselves well out of it.

My pride does not lie in exposing life unnecessarily; I have a natural disinclination to drowning; I think it my duty to preserve myself as long as possible, to amuse my fellow-citizens, and make them love nature and think of her as I do; and I take a higher satisfaction in remembering that, when I was coxswain, or had command, either in a boat or in any capacity, I never permitted myself to expose life out of bravado.

One may have a pride in bearing to be called timid; there is no place where young sailors are more apt to be over confident than in a boat. They will often attempt what whalemen and beach-combers would not attempt without trained crews. So generally is this the case, that I would caution any traveller who thinks his life a trust of some importance, not to go on boat expeditions among the surf, unless in a boat with a careful man who shall be captain for the occasion, and whose courage and skill does not require constant airing.

Some of the detached rocks on the seaward side of the North island, were very remarkable, both for size and shape. One of them cannot easily be forgotten by any who ever saw it. If painted upon the drop scene on the stage, where the decorators of the theatre usually indulge their fancies, it would be thought extravagant. Its form was that of two craggy arches forty feet high, crossing each other and uniting at the top, so as to form a natural open temple with four equidistant pillars. Its summit was usually tenanted by a solemn assembly of pelicans, who may have been, for aught a spectator knew, taking into consideration the condition of the crow population of the United States. I never passed this rock without regretting that I was not an artist; indeed the islands everywhere often awakened a similar regret—as will in a few years be believed, when commerce and the increased facilities for travel shall have afforded some of our artists an opportunity to open the wonderful and beautiful scenery of Peru to their countrymen.

But the sea lions, the hereditary lords of the islands, are as strange and remarkable as the grottoes. They are almost always swimming and blowing about among the shipping, and one soon gets tired of watching their movements. They may be seen in pairs and parties of all numbers up to twenty or thirty—rarely alone. They cruise leisurely around, swimming just under the surface, sticking their noses out and taking breath at irregular intervals; sometimes they do this as often as once in ten seconds, coming up as they swim, about once in a ship's length for several minutes in succession. This appears to be when they are "prospecting," as the miners would say, for a school of mackerel or herring. When they have gone on for a considerable distance in this way, either making a straight wake or winding about, they will sound and be gone much longer. In doing this they always turn on their sides and go down a back summerset like the pelicans in the air. I have seen them do this almost under the ship's stern within a few yards distance, in a calm forenoon when the water was like glass. Looking directly down upon them they use their flippers so like arms that they seem like devils in half human forms; I remember it made me shudder to see them turn and plunge directly down in the clear water, with such swiftness that in a second their forms were lost in the depth and darkness.

But of all created things and monsters in the world, I think there can be none that when seen near at hand wears so horrible a face and shape. Their mouths, with their enormous tusks or fangs, and cat-like whiskers, resemble somewhat the mouths of lions; their nostrils or blow-holes are very large, and they have great saucer-like eyes and no ears. To see them come up half out of water near a boat is positively awful to behold, and enough to shake any unaccustomed nerves. We chased a party of them one afternoon and tried to head them off and throw a lance into one, but they took good care to keep just out of reach. They were fishing, and several times they came up with mackerel in their teeth very near us. I never saw or dreamed of anything more horrid to look at. Their eyes are probably adapted to seeing at many fathoms depth, and from their staring I suspect they do not see well in the sunlight above. Nothing can be conceived more unnaturally hideous. They are the embodiment of despair. Along with the look of fierceness and cruelty, they have one of agony and suffering that makes them altogether appear to be the compelled agents of some diabolical spell or inevitable doom, like the wicked afrites and genies of the Arabian Nights.

Everything about them is mysterious. Half beast and half fish preying under water, living in darkness, and permitting themselves to be seen only partially, at brief intervals, and in shapes of such fearful ugliness—I could never wholly divest myself of the idea that they were animated by fiendish intelligences—that they were either possessed by devils or lost souls imprisoned in and made subject to the appetites of the most repulsive and voracious bodies.

Their breathing is always like sobbing ; their cries are wails; who knows what they could reveal if they could speak? The depths of the sea and the monstrous creatures that inhabit there are familiar to them, and so are the darkest recesses of the great caverns. They were created to be Destroyers. There is no doubt that to support their lives they must devour an incredible number of the small fishes. They may be seen for hours daily, chasing herring and mackerel, and evidently havocking among them right and left. When they are surfeited they retire to their caverns and lie stupidly on the slippery rocks till hunger drives them out to forage again.

On the leeward side of the middle island, there is a cavern a hundred yards across at the entrance, extending in more than twice as far, or at least accessible that far, in very calm times, by boats. Here may always be found sea lions reposing, and it is the chief ambition of captains and mates who love sport, to get in there among them. We could never find it calm enough to go in, though we *saw* in several times, and saw the creatures inward and outward bound as they passed us.

One of our Marblehead mates had been there, and was not a little proud of having killed his sea lion. There is some danger, if one slips on the rock or gets between the animals and the sea; they do not act on the offensive; and hideous as he is to the sight, a few heavy blows on the nose generally seals your seal's fate, and makes you owner of a huge carcass, sometimes nearly as large as a horse's, covered with a coarse hairy skin like india rubber when dried, and only valuable as a gift to Mr. Barnum, who may possibly use it in the manufacture of mermaids.

While I am speaking of Marblehead and mackerel, I must mention a curious development of instinct in some Cape Ann boys we had aboard ship. Not even the sea lions were more eager after the mackerel than they were. Every hour of their liberty they always employed in fishing. They cared not to go ashore, but let them have the yawl and their jigs and lines, and they were in clover. I almost pitied them sometimes, when after working all the week, they would stay off all Sunday, and return at night, burnt and fatigued, and as proud of a barrel of fish, more or less, as miss with a new bonnet.

But then I reflected that it was necessary for them to fish for mackerel in order to keep healthy; with them, fishing is the condition of their being; birds fly, beasts walk, men talk, Cape Ann boys *fish*. It is a strong argument in favor of the supposition that the animate creation as well as man, shall enjoy an immortality. For it cannot be supposed that all Marblehead is to be damned, whatever may be the case with an adjacent city; but a Marblehead fisherman cannot be in perfect bliss except he is fishing; therefore, and if peradventure there be any righteous persons in that village, there must be mackerel in the "superior spheres."

I must not forget the whales which came very frequently among the islands; nor omit to record, not boastingly, after the manner of some of our summer tourists, who make such an ado over their trouts and minnows, but incidentally merely, that I was one of a party who chased them in two boats, one the only whale boat in the fleet, for half an afternoon. I can almost see in my mind's eye, at least one of the companions of my youth, my old neighbor and friend, the best part of whose days were spent in cruising in the Pacific, reading this, and glorying in my "spunk." I can hear him laugh as he could do in former days when we used to sail down the bay to see him off on his three years' voyages. Little thought we then that our callings in life would ever be so reversed. But I shall make my boast now, if ever I see him again, that I have been after whales *since* he has. I did not get much oil, it is true; my "lay" was only that of a passenger; and worst of all, though we were well provided with all the conveniences, we could not succeed in "laying the boats on" so as to strike the game. Still it is something to have chased whales, and got *almost* near enough for the bowman to have thrown an iron into one of them; the fact must not be withheld in case I should ever visit Nantucket.

I was, in truth, particularly excited by the whales. They were the first I had ever seen in three oceans that realised the ideal. At sea, one has pointed out to him sometimes afar off, a thin spirt upon the blue water, which he is told is the spout of a whale; and that is all. He never sees them, or at least, I never saw them, rolling and breaching, or doing anything they are usually represented as doing in the drawings of them. We were, it is true, favored with a fin-back one day in the Pacific; we saw a portion of his back, and the fin upon it, but that only awakened curiosity to see more. At the Chinchas, on several occasions, my expectations were gratified, and fully realized; though no engraving that ever I saw, gives a correct idea of the shape or motions of the creature. We were, that afternoon, within twenty yards of them three or four times when they came up to blow; I could see the roughnesses on their mighty backs; they were large sperm whales, and they blew straight spouts thirty feet high, at least. Another, one evening, leaped clear from the water close by the ship; he was much longer, and better adapted for speed than the prints represent them; he blew like a steam engine—but I could have wished myself to windward of him. Their breath is almost insupportably fœtid.

Turtle are also plenty in the bay of Pisco. A large one

gave us a good view of himself as he passed along one calm morning under the ship's counter. They were brought over in boats from Pisco, and could be had at such a low price, that soup was no luxury.

"And a good south-wind sprung up behind;
The ALBATROSS did follow,"—

IV.

Guano, as I have stated in a preceding page, lies upon all the islands in the form of high, smooth, rounded hills, and covers nearly every part of all of them, following the inequalities of the underlying rock. At a distance it makes them all seem to be islands of rock, bordered by cavernous perpendicular cliffs, and covered with reddish yellow sand, but little lighter in color than the volcanic sand, which everywhere on hills and plains fringes the Peruvian coast. Where it has been cut away it is lighter still, being of an undecided mixture of red, white, yellow and gray—a sort of subochre, or to be very precise, about the color of white and red ashes of anthracite coal, mingled in equal proportions. On the sides of the cuttings where it has been taken away, it may be seen to lie in separately colored layers or strata, generally parallel with the plane of the horizon, of all thicknesses from that of a sheet of pasteboard to two or three inches; the red layers were usually the thickest; but they were of all shades and succeeded each other without any ascertainable order—red, white, brownish, grayish, faint yellow, earthy, white, brown, red, and so on—so that I could never adopt a theory which I much wished to form, that the differently colored strata were deposits made at different seasons, year after year, for ages, and that each season had a peculiar correspondent hue on account of the periodical visits of different species of birds, or of birds and seals.

Indeed, although interested in the inquiry, as no one could help being in so singular a place, I was never able to satisfy myself with any hypothesis to account for the guano being there as it is under all its conditions. That it is produced by birds and seals there can be no doubt. Every part of it abounds with the remains of them. Eggs, and wing bones of birds, and canine teeth of sea lions changed to ammonia, are found in every part of it; I cut them out with my knife from the base of the cutting on the North island, where the guano is deepest, a hundred and fifty feet below the surface. After going down a few feet, the whole substance of the stratified deposit is the same throughout. In some places there is a difference in depth of color perceptible in contiguous strata for a foot or two in thickness, extending along the whole of the cuttings where they are exposed. This would include so many of the thin strata, that it must have taken years, and perhaps hundreds of years, in its formation. What causes could have operated to give so marked a change of color, while the producing and stratifying agencies were unchanged, through so long a time? Why should a series of strata, the same in substance and form, be redder or browner than other series above and below it? I could no more account for this than for the irregularity of the strata themselves.

Buried in the guano, also at great depths, are fragments of granite, not water worn, but freshly fractured, like fragments thrown off in blasting and chipping. They occur in pieces so large that birds or seals could never have brought them there; there is no granite nearer than San Gallan Island, nearly twenty miles to the southward. How shall we account for their being there?

But what was most puzzling, the strata do not follow the convexity of the hills. They are more level. And I remarked in the only place where the cuttings gave an opportunity for observing, that they continued at nearly the same level on two elevations, and did not follow the depression of an inconsiderable valley. They cropped out on the sides of one swell or gentle roll of the surface and appeared on another, as if the intervening depression had been worn away by the action of water. But how, if the guano has been for the last few centuries in process of formation by birds and seals, should these out-cropping strata come out so near the surface? for I should have observed that the edges of the layers on the sides of the elevations come out to within a few feet, and mingle there with loose unstratified guano, which forms a surface covering everywhere. If the horizontal strata had been submerged and worn away by water into elevations and depressions, as seemed the only reasonable supposition, why should not the constantly forming deposit, in the ages since its emergence, take the form of the mounds and valleys on which it rests? We cannot suppose that the islands have changed their form in the last hundred years; in that time one would think that new strata would have been formed which would have overlaid the other like a rind. But the level strata include all the compact guano, and preserve their places nearly to the height of the elevations. It is true that the seals are said to have resorted to the highest places they could find, and their skeletons may still be seen on the summit of the South Island, at least four hundred feet above the sea level. This might in part account for the apparent out-cropping of the strata; the seals might have preferred the elevations and deserted the depressions, and the strata might thus appear to have been abraded by water after deposition. This was the only supposition; and the strata were so strongly marked, and the undulations of the surface so gentle, that it was far from satisfactory.

That such great deposits could have been formed by seals and birds alone, is not at all incredible; it is only the conditions under which they are found that are so difficult to account for—the irregularity in the order of the strata, the difference in color in contiguous series of strata in the almost homogeneous mass, the presence of fragments of granite, and the apparent independence of the strata and want of conformity with the inequalities of the surface. Here would seem to be enough inexplicable phenomena, without opening the inquiry how such masses of ammonia could have remained under water, on the supposition of their submergence.

On each of the three Chinchas is a place where the uniformity of the cliffs is interrupted, and the hill of guano slopes down to a narrow beach. It was said by English captains and others who had visited the islands fifteen or twenty years ago, that thousands—millions, one of them expressed it—of seals, might then be seen going up these slopes at certain times of the year to the tops of the hills. On the south island I saw many skeletons of them lying on the surface or half buried in it, and fancied I could trace where the bodies had turned, and what was left of them was still turning to guano. The animals must have reached there of their own accord, though why they should choose to ascend so high out of their usual element on a hot dusty hill, and how they were able to drag themselves over it nearly a mile and four or five hundred feet upward, are points on which they have not left us any information. But the fact is unquestionable, and is another singularity in the natural history of these mysterious creatures. If they invaded the high land in such numbers as is related, the largest portion of the guano may be readily accounted for. Multitudes were left there dead; the old sealers frequently say that it is for this purpose alone, to die, that the creatures ascended. The vestiges of such hosts must have been enormous. The sea lion is a consumer and producer on a most magnificent scale, as well as a practical free-trader; there is no tariff on his imports and exports. Coprophagous birds must have accompanied his progress in myriads; the turkey-buzzards must have hung over his dying carcass like the breath of the sweet south, and the vultures of the sea must have hovered and flapped around him, shaking a thousand odors from their dewy wings.

The result of all my investigations of this delicate subject, is that the reddish streaks in the guano are from small birds and the remains of sea lions, which the vultures could not carry away; the other lighter colored strata, generally thinner, are from pelicans and the larger sea birds. There is nothing in the way of the supposition, that the whole deposit may have been formed long since the building of the Pyramids of the Nile, except the granite fragments and the water-worn valleys; and I am inclined to think it of recent formation, notwithstanding these. Very little decay or loss takes place after the vultures have done their work and the chemical action changing the tough hides and bones to ammonia has begun. The climate is so dry that the volatile alkali is not set free, but remains there forever Perhaps the granite fragments were thrown there in some of the eruptions that may have occurred on this coast, within the last thousand years; but then they are found through the whole substance. No sea lions now visit the islands large enough to have carried them there. Perhaps, too, the islands have been submerged, or great waters have flowed over them in earthquakes, such as destroyed old Callao; and perhaps not. Fortunately travellers are not obliged to account for all the unexplained phenomena they meet with. I shall therefore leave the subject with the usual Spanish "*Quien sabe?*" It may have been already investigated; if not, it should be brought to the notice of scientific men as a curious inquiry.

I wish I could see it treated of by such a writer as the author of the "Geology of the Exploring Expedition," a work which, so far as a general reader may judge, presents splendid examples of acute observation and philosophical generalization.

The pungent odor of guano is not found unpleasant

after one is a little accustomed to it. It is by no means a filthy substance; not so much so as common soil. In washing the hands, it has a half-soapy feel, and leaves them readily. It whitens ropes and rigging after repeated rains have washed them. On board ship, during the voyage, we perceive nothing of it except when the wind is directly aft, and creates a calm in the cabin and between-decks. But when loading, ships are covered with it and its odor, and the fine dust of it penetrates everywhere, and has the property of tarnishing brass and silver. We thought it must be healthy; for we ate like sea-lions at the Chinchas. I often wondered our stomachs did not burst. The increase of appetite was generally attributed to the vivifying properties of the guano. But the climate must have some of the praise. To my apprehension, that was altogether, everything delightful and salubrious. Yet when I think of the system that is maintained there, the hard fate of the poor wretches who dig the guano, and all the circumstances of obtaining cargoes, the islands seem to me to be a kind of human *abattoir*, or slaughter-house of men; and I feel a relief in being away from them, as one feels who has escaped out of some gloomy dream.

V.

At the north island, on board a miserable hulk or guard ship, is stationed a commandant and a few soldiers of the Callao pattern, a portion of whom act as sentry and watch on the island itself, where, on the north cliff, is the official residence of a deputy commandant, SERRATE, and his subordinates. This is the head quarters of the Peruvian authorities at the Islands. SERRATE is the chief person with whom captains have to deal, and is superior to KOSSUTH, though that enterprising individual, who knows many secrets, and among them some that SERRATE would not wish to have published, maintains an independence *de facto*, if not *de jure*. The limits of the actual authority of each were never ascertained. Probably if the truth was known, the two lay their heads together and collude, (or as a down-east client of a legal acquaintance used to read, "conudle,") about the division of the spoil. How all their business is managed—why some ships are obliged to lie at the north island and others at the middle, why they are often obliged to move from one to the other, and how it is that some get loaded before their lay days expire, while others have to be paid demurrage, are phenomena which admit of a very obvious explanation. The captains, who must be supposed to know, universally attribute such seeming caprices of Messrs. Serrate and Kossuth to the influence of money to them severally in hand paid—to bribes. As it is not possible for all to secure a preference at once by this means, the system naturally creates no little discontent among the captains, whose owners may refer its unavoidable partiality to lack of good management. But so must business be conducted in Peru.

The guano is dug from the hills, and wheeled to depots or open enclosures, called "Mangueras," on the edge of the cliffs, at places where launches or vessels can be moored below—by coolies, who are brought to Peru by English ships from the free ports of China. There are about three hundred coolies at work on the middle island, and seven or eight hundred on the north. It is said that they are brought here under contracts made with them at home, to labor for five years, at a real, or York shilling, per day, and their rice; and that after they have served their time out they are free to return. It is said, also, that they are induced to come by being made to believe they are going to labor in gold mines. The real truth I suppose to be, that they are contracted for by the Peruvian Government, and transferred to it, at a good profit, by the English who bring them. Whatever their contracts may be, if there are any, the coolies, who are one of the contracting parties, become, in effect, absolutely slaves. They are condemned to be diggers of guano; their labor is much more severe and injurious than railroad digging; they have no liberty days, no protecting laws, no power to obtain even the pittance said to be paid them, no proper seasons of rest. Most of them go nearly naked; none have more than enough clothing just to cover themselves; they live and feed like dogs; they are constantly within reach of the thongs of hideous black drivers—the link between men and devils; there are no women among them, nothing to mitigate their hopeless toil. Before and around them is the shining bay, and beyond it green groves and mountains; near at hand hundreds of ships coming and going, filled with men like themselves, only free! They, too, have been free; they were not born in slavery; they are not domestic slaves or plantation slaves: but slaves without any title, or rights, or conceded customs—mere over-worked beasts of burden.

Almost every week some of them commit suicide by throwing themselves from the cliff. They are said to do this in the belief that their spirits will awaken in their native land. Kossuth told me that more than sixty had killed themselves this way in the two years he has been there. One was driven over the cliff or jumped off, and was dashed in pieces, to escape the lash of a black driver, who chased him to the verge in sight of a captain of an American ship, the week before we left. The cliff where he leaped is two hundred feet high, and almost perpendicular. Kossuth affects to pity these coolies; but he is said to over-task them. Each one, strong and weak alike under his overseers, is required to dig and wheel to the mangueras, five tons of guano per day. They are kept at labor Sundays as well as other days; under Serrate, however, on the North Island, I believe Sundays are allowed them —or, at least, they are said to be paid a little extra if they choose to dig guano on that day

On this island, also, a steam "paddy" is employed in the digging, and the guano is brought to the principal manguera in dirt-carts on rails, as it is at one of them on Kossuth's island. Here also is a sort of cane-shanty hospital, and various other shed-like houses, groceries, cookery, carpenter-shop, and the like, making in all quite a village or collection of hovels, inhabited by interpreter, doctors, overseers, drivers, cholo women, and nondescripts in ragged ponchos. I spent a night or two here with a medical gentleman; everything was guano, but we smoked paper cigarettoes, and said "Que cuidar?" and made ourselves intelligible to each other in broken Spanish mended with worse Latin. I was satisfied with a very cursory examination of the internal economy of Senor Serrates' kingdom.

Towards the cliff, along the lee side of each island, the surface has a steep slope; on this are placed the mangueras, which reach to the edge of the cliff. These mangueras are large enclosures made of strong canes somewhat resembling the palisade round our prisons. They are supported, as they stand on the inclined rock, by chain cables, four to each, which pass round them at different heights, and are secured above. Into them the guano is brought by wheelbarrows and dirt cars, drawn by donkeys, from the sides of the hill where it is cut away. Coolies, who are obliged to wear thick bandages over their mouths, push the guano down to the lower ends of the mangueras, where there are openings connected with "shutes," or long canvas pipes, about as large round as barrels, that lead down to the bases of the cliff. Through these the guano is conducted into launches, or directly into the holds of vessels loading. When thus taken in by launches, it has to be hoisted in over the ship's side in sacks or tubs, by a tackle and fall, a work requiring several weeks to complete a cargo. When poured directly into ships, moored for the purpose under rocks, it takes but a day or two. In either case the ship is all over guano from stem to stern. Awnings and sails are spread over the after decks, and everything is covered that can be, but to little purpose. Many ships parcel their standing rigging from the dead-eyes up to the ends of the shrouds, to prevent the guano from getting in among the lanyards; but it is generally thought to be a needless precaution. While "loading at the shutes," ships are moored alongside, parallel with the face of the rocks, and only a few feet from them. Outside they are kept off by hawsers attached to buoys anchored for the purpose. The water is so bold that the heaviest vessels can thus be moored within four or five fathoms of the cliff. It is enough to make one nervous to see them lying so near, for on surf days the heave of the sea is felt around under the lee of the islands, and vessels thus moored would often roll their lower yards against the rocks, if they were not cock-billed. I remember spending a night on board a large clipper, riding only by a single hawser attached to the chain of the buoy, and drifting scarcely a ship's length from the precipice, at the mouth of a cave that was roaring all night, and made the black rocks seem like wild creatures longing to get at us. But then a wind which would have brought a strain upon the hawser would have been almost as miraculous as the strong wind of Egypt.

When the guano is pouring down the shute into a ship's hold, she is as completely enveloped and hidden in the yellow smoke of it as if she were on fire with a cargo of lard. The ammonia is so strong that it is like entering a bottle of hartshorn to go into her interior—eyes and nose and lungs are all assailed at once. How the Cholos breathe and survive their labor as "trimmers," to distribute the guano in the hold, where it is so thick as to be almost dark, is marvellous. They work with "muzzles," or thick bandages over their mouths, and almost naked.

When a ship has got her cargo or comes out from under the shute, the crew hoist the national flag, and send up one of their number in a tub to the yard-arm, where he leads off in three cheers, which are answered by the crews of all the vessels lying near, more especially by those of the same nation. It is animating to hear the cheer taken up, and echoed as it often is through the entire fleet. Of the English vessels, many make the voyage exclusively for the guano, and do not take it as ours do for a return freight. Their crews are shipped for the voyage, and do not consist of cholos. All the poor fellows have some reason for rejoicing when they get through their disagreeable task of loading.

The Coolies who dig the guano are brought here in English vessels—the fact is notorious. I have often conversed with English captains who spoke freely of having been engaged in the traffic. Whatever may be the engagement of the Coolies, and if there be any, it is characterized by fraudulent representations and bad faith in the other party, their transporters and those who transfer them to the Peruvian government, know that *they* are engaged in a slave trade as much as if they brought slaves from Africa.

For argument sake and to smooth over the matter, they of course can urge a "contract," "apprenticeship," "that the Coolies are as well off here as at home," and the like; but speaking as among men of the world, all the world knows that they sell the Coolies into slavery—and they cannot give it any other name that will make it smell sweeter. It is, moreover, the worst and most cruel slavery of all forms of slavery that exist among civilized nations. It was universally said to be so by captains who had visited every quarter of the globe; I am sure I never saw anything like it on the plantations, when I once resided for several months in the country adjoining that where the the scene of the popular tale of "Uncle Tom's Cabin" is laid.

It is not my purpose to insist on these facts in order to appeal to the feelings or awaken sympathy or indignation; a mere harmless sketch of travels is hardly the place for that. But I think such matters of public interest ought to be held up to the light. It may do English readers no harm to know that their countrymen are not absolutely immaculate. English writers are rather more ready to point out our faults than to help us amend them. Perhaps the *name* changes the *thing;* if it does not, why should not the English government send out cruisers with instructions to capture vessels of their own country laden with Coolies for this market? An American may, with peculiar propriety, make the suggestion; it is but a kind return for the sympathy Englishmen and women manifest for us in our troubles that we should hint to them where their own affairs would seem to claim prior attention—to say nothing of the natural satisfaction there is in it.

VI.

I AM glad I have done with the Chinchas, and the Guano, and the Coolies. The islands themselves are in the highest degree wonderful and picturesque; the formation of the guano is a fruitful subject for curious speculation, but it was dusty, and there was something too much of it; and the Coolies and their fate impart a gloomy coloring to the recollection of the whole time spent there. I seem to see them at their work, their slender figures quivering under the weight of loads too heavy for them to wheel; for every one who went ashore remarked that they took loads altogether disproportioned to their apparent strength, which was generally accounted for by saying "how much stronger those fellows are than they look ?" But then everywhere among them are huge negroes, blacker than the ten of spades, who walk about with heavy thongs, such as they drive donkeys with, which they are laying on the naked backs of the Coolies in one or another part of the diggings almost constantly. I never went ashore at the middle island without witnessing this operation, and hearing the cries of the sufferers. I observed Coolies shovelling and wheeling as if for dear life, and yet their backs were covered with great welts. The negroes did not look capable of either justice or mercy.

It is easy to distinguish Coolies who have been at the islands a short time from the new comers. They soon become emaciated, and their faces have a wild, despairing expression. That they are worked to death is as apparent as that the hack horses in our cities are used up in the same manner.

When I wrote a letter to the New York Times detailing some of the facts now narrated, I read it to several English captains, who said "You are rather hard upon us; but it cannot be denied; it is all true!" But England ought to be able to bear the truth, and from whom better than one whom certain of the baser sort (by which it is not meant Radicals exclusively) have long ago set down as a confirmed Anglomaniac. The reputation also of being a fair-minded and fair reporting observer is worth something.

If I were disposed to write as a philanthropist, the Coolie system would afford an excellent theme; it was tried in Australia but proved unprofitable. But my benevolence does not feel called upon to develope itself that way. It is enough for me if I can aid in spreading a love of nature and a taste for the arts; some "also serve, who only stand and wait." The philanthropists can hardly claim one who thinks it would be a greater benefit to America if the negro minstrelsy could be supplanted by some stronger popular music among our white people, than if all the blacks were at once emancipated. Besides, I do not approve of the crying school in literature.

But there is an annoying class of English who are often met with in our cities, who are slightly deficient in modesty, as well as thoroughly convinced that they have a right to say anything, and that everything they say, or that London says, must be so. Perhaps the Chinchas may supply a convenient argument for a boarding-house breakfast table.

On shipboard the time passes at the islands much more agreeably than might be supposed. The captains visit each other, and spin interminable yarns, and "talk ship," and enjoy society with the natural zest of men much deprived of it. The conversation of men who have seen so much of the world is always interesting; it is hearing books of travel *talked.* There is a life and reality in the actual telling of things, relating anecdotes of foreign customs and manners, and describing scenes in distant countries, which cannot be conveyed in writing. It has imperceptibly something the same effect that visiting those countries would have; it loosens the soil around one, and allows him to expand. The individual *ego*, that obtrusive personage of whom every one is more or less weary, loses his importance, and what he has done and suffered is of less consequence than he would have have had us imagine. Even the world itself no longer surrounds us with such a mighty mystery; we find that our little corner was not the whole of it—that men live who think very differently from our philosophers—that the limits of the actual and the ideal are much the same everywhere. A student of himself, and true lover of nature, ought to be made more assured, and more liberal minded by the society of sea-faring men. Their roughness is oftenest, like that of the ocean, only external, and they are as free as the wind. I have often thought how must the world appear to one whose whole life has been spent in going round and over it; probably not larger than a globe used in a school-room. Only circumnavigating it once, and surveying mankind from Australia to Peru, diminishes it very materially.

Nor are shipmasters at all disposed to be exclusive or reserved to any one who lets himself out freely and acts and talks in a manly fashion. Most of them are quick to find out what a passenger is made of, and whether he wishes to make himself agreeable and comfortable or otherwise. Their profession, more than almost any other, leads them to consider the social qualities of man. Life on shipboard, brings out men's dispositions. Montaigne writes an essay on "the inconvenience of greatness;" the captain of any American ship full of passengers to the gold regions, can appreciate how much may be said upon that theme. Instead of being rash and sudden in temper, as they are sometimes imagined to be, our captains ought to be regarded as miracles of patient endurance.

So far, therefore, as intercourse with intelligent men of the world could make time pass pleasantly, no one need have felt the want of it at the islands; though there was a passenger on a ship that lay near us, who seldom left his state-room during the two months the ship lay there, except at meal-times. There were several ladies, who sometimes participated in the boat excursions, the wives and daughters of captains in the fleet; I remember seeing at the same table three, from New, and Old England, and Scotland, respectively.

Most of those who can, generally make a visit of a few days over to Pisco, the town which gives its name to the bay. This is directly across the bay eastwardly about fourteen miles. A few miles further round in the bight of the bay, is a fishing village, or collection of cane huts, called Paracca, beyond which Paracca point, a high volcanic promontory, comes round ten miles to the southward and eastward of the island. San Gallan, an island eight hundred feet high, stands out from it in the Pacific three or four miles westward. The coast around all the eastern shore of the bay, is flat and sandy for many miles inland. Only a few green patches of trees, and the white trace of the sunburnt houses of Pisco, are all that can be seen from the islands, of vegetation or human presence; and the landscape is but little improved when seen close at hand. On the side where the town is situated, a mile inland from the beach, the bay shoals so much that the beach cannot be approached within half a mile, except in light boats; and the landing is difficult on account of the surf, which is sometimes very heavy. There are few houses on the beach, and a sort of custom house, or government warehouse.

Pisco contains from four to five thousand inhabitants, and is quite an important Peruvian town. It is built, like Callao, of huts, and one and two-story adobe or mud-walled houses, in narrow streets, regularly laid out, and has several plazas or open squares, the principal of which contains the market. There are three or four churches—one of which, on the market square, is the most conspicuous building in the town. A few miles out is a large sugar plantation, occupying a thousand acres or more, enclosed by a high adobe wall, and containing houses and gardens. This estate is owned by a company in Lima, and is kept in cultivation by the labor of about five hundred slaves. The brown sugar of Peru has something the flavor of ma ple sugar; partially refined it resembles very dirty loaf sugar. A large proportion of the produce of sugar estates is converted into spirits. The distilling of the commonest sort of liquor is the principal business of Pisco, and 'pisco' is hence the name of the liquor throughout the country. It has something the flavor and appearance of the cheapest sort of gin. Another sort called Italia, is somewhat better —it has a more fruity flavor, and is sold at a higher price. For aught I know, it may be made from the grape. Both these liquors are put up for transportation, not in wood, but in large unglazed earthen jars from two to four feet high, and shaped like tops—a form which seems at first the most inconvenient that could be thought of, since they cannot stand alone. But they are not ill adapted for being carried one on each side of a mule, in a country where casks must be dear, and roads are only paths among mountains. Long droves of mules laden with them and other produce, such as hay and coarse wheat, are seen daily coming into Lima and Callao.

Forty miles inland from Pisco, or half-way to the Andes, is Ica, a rural town of some ten thousand inhabitants, and four or five times as many women as men. They are chiefly occupied in cultivating the vine, and are said to be very well pleased to be visited by strangers, of whom they see but few. The accounts of the climate there, and the fruits and wine, the amiable disposition, and beauty, and graces of the maidens, their dances, and all that—would make the valley of Ica a Peruvian Arcady. But the school-master, when he visits these regions, will find himself solitary there; he will long for the " respite and nepenthe"— the social intercourse that alone can quiet the restless mind, and without which the world is everywhere a desert. I should, I am sure.

THE BAY OF PISCO.

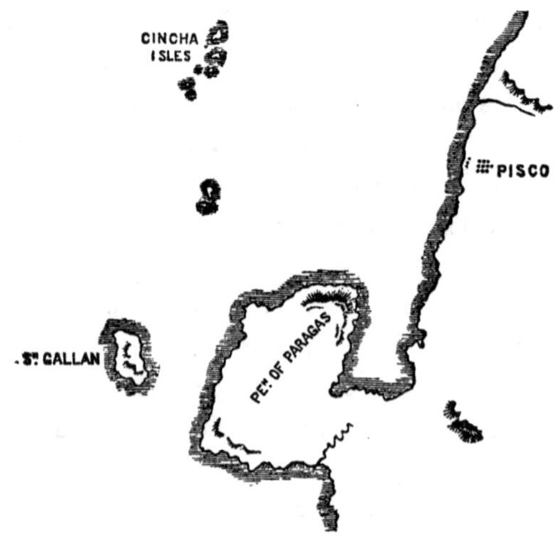

VI.

We sailed from the Chinchas on the 10th of November. It was a still, hazy morning—so still that the Tornado hung by warps passed out to other ships lying near after her anchor was weighed and her principal sails loosed. She had taken the last of her cargo from the shute and from launches at the north end of the North Island, so that she was almost the last vessel towards the sea, and clear of everything after getting her anchor. I had come round from the Middle Island to join her three days before, in order to be in readiness; but on account of the state she was in, had accepted an invitation to remain on board the Simoon, which lay near by, until her departure. The Simoon was another magnificent clipper, with a deck on which a regiment of infantry might have been drilled. It was almost a pity to see the preparations making on board her to receive the guano, and to fancy what a condition she would be in while loading. We remained walking her deck till the Tornado began to move slowly seaward, when we got into a boat and went alongside, Captain Smith of the Simoon, Captain Burgess of the Governor Morton, and myself. We found several captains, American and English, on the quarter-deck, it being the custom for captains to visit and shake hands at parting, as it is to pilot each other in.

There were many whose acquaintance made me regret leaving the Chinchas. I hope these lines may meet the eyes of some of the old sea-lions, (captains are all "old men," behind their backs, aboard ship) and that they will not have forgotten me. Some of them are almost public enough to be mentioned by name; but the list is too long. John ———, I have seen thine in Gleason's Pictorial, accompanying a view of the launch of thy noble ship—the same woodcut which had already in all probability appeared in the character of several of McKay's clippers. Thou who wast acknowledged the strongest and the best natured fellow in college, and whom every one of the old boys will remember for those qualities, I will mention thee to let them know that "age has not withered thee," as any one may find to his cost who trusts his fingers within that mass of muscle thou callest a hand. I smiled inwardly when thou informedst me that thou "never had any trouble with men; never struck one in your life; doubted if you could knock one down." The man thou shouldst hit, John, would not have time to fall; his fate would in one particular resemble the translation of Enoch, who walked and "was not;" he would vanish like Ariel into the elements, and leave not a rack behind; we should not know where to look for him!

While the captains were exchanging farewells, the ship was gathering way and the crew were making sail. About two o'clock the boats left us, and the royals and skysails began to feel the light air. The sun was well down when the Chinchas faded from the horizon, and the stars came out over the gently-heaving Pacific. Through the night, the air continued light, but the ship seemed to be moved onward by a spirit that slid "nine fathom deep" beneath her keel. In the morning we made land to windward of Chincha Head, forty miles below San Lorenzo. The decks and deck-houses, and coils of rigging, were covered with guano, and the first washing down the decks converted the whole into yellow soapy mud. We were all that morning in a "regular mess." Indeed it was not till we had been a week at sea after leaving Callao on the voyage home, that the ship was comfortably clean; and her upper spars and tackle were yellow till we got into the rainy weather of the latitude of Patagonia.

LIMA.

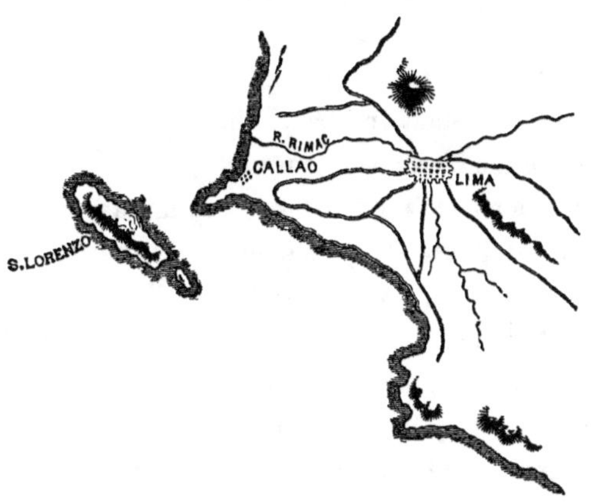

By five in the afternoon, we were at anchor in Callao Roads, having run down in a day a distance which it takes often a fortnight for vessels to make in beating up. There were nearly a hundred vessels lying in the roads, bound to and from the Chinchas; a few of them I had seen at Melbourne.

The sunset was clear, as all sunsets are in that delicious climate, and we lay so near the beach at the mouth of the river, that we could see the children bathing. The green line of trees reached far along the shore, and the white towers of the churches of Lima, lay beyond the green in a distant line at the feet of the mountains. The green of the tropics is like that of early spring; the very shade of color gives a sense of freshness. The mountains are burnt and bare, and rise abruptly from the plain, so high that one is never sure that he sees the highest of them. As the sun descends, the yellow summits come out above each other more and more distant and hazy, till they are hidden by the shadow of the ocean, and it is night.

The plain is almost a dead level, ten miles across and twenty in length, ascending gradually from the sea. Lima lies in the bight of it, seven miles from Callao and several hundred feet higher, though the ascent is so gradual as not to be perceptible. Beyond, the plain extends upward and becomes a valley in the mountains, down which comes the river Rimac, which flows through and waters the city and empties into the bay a mile north of Callao.

The site of Lima is worthy of the "City of Kings." (*Cindad de los Reyes.*) The broad plain, overshadowed and enclosed by the dark mountains, has the features of a place consecrated by antiquity and historic associations. The mountains look down upon it like guardian giants, and the towers and temples of the city rise above its green expanse, recalling the palaces of Atabalipa. The whole scene has an atmosphere of nobleness, and splendor, and vague magnificence, which no familiarity can dispel.

The morning after our arrival I went ashore, and found Callao still standing where it did, though we had heard at the Chinchas that it had been severely shaken by an earthquake some time in October—the month in which such phenomena most frequently occur. Nothing was changed, except that the sun had grown a little hotter. There were the same shipchandlers' shops, the same groups of captains, the same knots of sailors, the same tawdrily dressed Cholo and Zambo girls, the same formidable display of soldiers.

The railroad depot is at the very end of the mole; it is much like a large unbuilt building composed of high mud pilasters not half finished, and without any roof! The foot-path to it leads through an army of pisco jars standing on end against each other. On one side is a large heap of wheat, which in this rainless climate requires no housing; a shanty on the top of it contains a negro family, whether placed there to improve the flavosity of the wheat, or prevent it from being stolen, I did not inquire.

The railroad leads round the castle, and along the left of the site of "old Callao," (overwhelmed by an earthquake wave, in 1746,) which lies between it and the sea. I walked over this melancholy place more than once. It is mostly a plain of heaps of gravel, volcanic cinders, and burnt earth. Here and there in many parts, the ruins of brick walls and arches appear above the surface. I looked down several arch-ways and hollows that were strewn with bones and human skulls. They are thrown there for effect or convenience, and were not exhumed. The sea buried its victims too deep for that.

II.

The cars run to and from Lima every two hours during the day; the fare is half a dollar in the first class and a quarter in the second, for a ride of about twenty minutes. The first class are divided in compartments, holding six each; the second are open boxes. The cars, as well as the engines, are all English built. The trains appear always full; on fete days, of which there are a great many, they are crowded. The road must be very profitable. It has only been built a few years, and the people have not done admiring the wonderful plaything. As I rode up and down sometimes in the open cars, I often fancied I could see the looks of astonishment on the contenances of native Peruvians, whose rustic ways and dusty ponchos, proclaimed them strangers to the sights of commerce; they were doubtless visiters from Pisco, Ica, or the interior towns.

The road goes for two miles straight over a miserable burnt plain, exhibiting only cane shanties, low mud fences, a few trees, droves of donkeys, cholo women with two braids of hair hanging down their backs, and with and without hats, riding astride on donkeys and horses, ragged negroes, and here and there mud ruins of nondescript structures, and prison like enclosures,—a vicinity all dreary dust and desolation. Gradually the cars skirt fields of Indian corn in all stages of growth, some ripening, some just springing from the ground, walled plantations of bananas, orange trees, and other fruits, crossed by little canals of swift-running water, trees resembling locust and willow, and a few roads for carriages winding among them. But there is no greensward, such as we see at home. The ground is all crumbly earth, like broken dry mud, and looks anything but fertile. Arrived in the suburb, the train goes slower through a long lane of mud cabins alive with negroes of all shades and sizes, and finally deposits its burden where there is a gateway leading into the principal *calle*, or main street of Lima.

This is a long, narrow, paved street, lined with low, gloomy two-story houses, clumsily built of adobes or mud.

Only a few of the newer ones have glazed windows in the second story. Most have narrow casements opening into blank walls or latticed verandahs, as represented in Wilkes, after the fashion of old Spain; indeed, almost every step in Lima reminded me of Cervantes and Le Sage. This street is a very old one, and reaches through the Arcade fronting the church in the grand Plaza, and thence under the gateway, (of which there is a very good engraving in Wilkes,) over the bridge and far on the other side, or nearly through the middle of the city. I remember reading a date 1731 carved on a granite post somewhere not very far from the depot. The street runs straight from the depot to the Arcade, and the sign of "Morin's," which is the principal commercial hotel, and is the first building of the Arcade on the corner of the Plaza, is visible from the gateway of the station-house, informing the public in very large characters and in plain English, that "Hot and Cold Baths" may be obtained there at all reasonable hours—not the fact, by the way, at the time of my visit, owing to temporary repairs. I enjoyed a lively flea bath one night, and the next adjourned to the "Boule d'Or" on the same street, where I was regaled with a similar luxury—but of the fleas enough. The three or four hotels, of which these are the best, with the exception of one in another street, which is rather a first-class boarding house than a hotel, are all in this street, near the Plaza. There are two churches upon it, and it exhibits the most showy retail shops; with the Arcades, which are wide piazzas covering the sidewalk and extending round three sides of the Plaza, it constitutes the Broadway of the city, though there are many other streets of shops, as well as many occupied by the better sort of dwellings.

Lima is chiefly laid out in squares, and the streets cross each other at right angles, except near the river, where they are accommodated to its partly diagonal course, as it flows through the city from East to West. They are narrow, and the pavement of them is ancient and uneven. The sidewalks are roughly flagged and extremely narrow. The streets slope from either sidewalk to gutters in the middle, which in all the east and west streets are open, swift running streams of water—a luxury almost as invaluable to Lima as the Croton to New York. These open sewers pass under every crossing, and have descent enough to carry off the various impurities poured into them very expeditiously. In the streets occupied by dwellings, the construction of the houses is such that one sees in looking down them, only alleys of yellow mud walls, with gateways or entrances for carriages. They look precisely like streets of stables. Only here and there a portico, with coarse, dingy, and rickety green blinds, overhangs the sidewalk. Very few buildings, except the churches and convents, and one store on a corner in the main street, not yet completed, are of more than two stories. Except on holiday occasions, there are few carriages; but there are always horses and donkeys without number. The water-carriers go about with narrow casks, holding about a third of a barrel, placed endwise one on each side of a donkey, while they ride astern; they are generally negroes, and their clothing, and the beasts, and their old rope trappings and panniers, make them seem at a little distance like animated masses of dusty sweepings. Besides these, there are strings of donkeys laden and almost hidden with loads of new hay, or rather green grass, so coarse that it resembles weeds; others with wood, earth for building, market vegetables, meats—every conceivable sort of stuff that donkeys can be made to carry. The corners of the streets are usually occupied by groceries, open to two streets, and with counters running crosswise; they resemble those which may be seen in the lowest quarters of our cities. I often inquired the way to the Plaza at them, and was always treated with politeness.

Except in the principal streets, there are not many people walking in the better parts of the city, and the absence of carriages makes them seem almost deserted. But as one passes along, he may look through the gateways across paved court-yards into the very parlors of the houses, which open within each other like the scenery in flat at the theatre. Often the family carriage stands on one side in the court; at the back is a spacious plainly-furnished hall, open through to a small garden or conservatory, the inner court of the house; beyond this may be seen the parlor, with its centre table and lamp, and red and white curtains —the whole open and arranged to produce a fine scenic effect from the street. Almost all the better houses are thus constructed, and under their gloomy exteriors conceal residences of apparently luxurious elegance within. The style is peculiarly adapted to the climate, and not a little tantalizing to the eye of a stranger as he wanders alone through the yellow sun-burnt lanes.

Not far from the railroad station, turning down two or three squares to the left, in a street which crosses the principal one, is the residence of Mr. Clay, the American Minister, which may be distinguished by the national escutcheon and a flagstaff above the gateway. The house is constructed in the usual style of the city. A narrow court intervenes between the street and a large open apartment, which leads directly through to the parlors and private rooms; on the left is the Minister's audience hall or office, where all Americans will be sure to find a courteous reception, and such information as may facilitate the accomplishment of their purposes in visiting the Peruvian capital. Mr. Clay is universally spoken of by Americans in Lima and Callao in terms of the highest respect, as a most worthy representative of our government. In a country like Peru, where changes of rulers take place almost every hour, and its political organization forever trembles on the verge of anarchy, his office can be no sinecure; his interference is often called for in the transactions of business, as well as in matters of state. The duties of the legation must be very laborious as well as often perplexing, and the Chincha exportation and all the affairs growing out of the employment of so much American capital, and the presence of so many American citizens in Peru, must have increased them very materially within a year or two.

A great portion of Lima is occupied by churches and convents, or held as the property of the Church. At first view, the churches, with their ancient and dingy cracked walls, and towers surmounted by pinnacles leaning in every direction, have a very mean appearance. But the eye soon accommodates itself to the intention of architectural effects. The narrow streets widen with the presence of the lively multitude, and the churches grow large and splendid. I was often surprised at the change, and even now can hardly account for the interior of churches appearing more spacious than those of halls and houses of worship at home which are much larger. But everything goes by comparison; where the streets are all narrow and the houses low, small churches look large, and short distances grow long. Some of the churches in Lima are really large; often, with the monasteries and convents attached, they cover whole squares, and form cities in themselves, of chapels and galleries and gardens, a complicated maze of buildings, where a foreigner could hardly walk alone without some apprehension that he might be caught and converted unawares, in the old inquisitorial mode.

The convents have high walls, and no windows on the street. Their gates are heavy and barred with an ostentation of seclusion, very melancholy to the eye of a free man, and suggestive of solemn thoughts. I cannot believe that the Church of Christ should encourage, if it should permit, men and women to take upon themselves, ever so willingly, such irrevocable vows; still less that it should enforce the assuming such unnatural obligations. I no more believe it than I believe in Shakerism or Mormonism. With a deference for ecclesiastical authority, little understood by most of my countrymen, and a speculative, if unfortunately not a lively faith in the church, and with a profound reverence for Christian art, I must yet, in some particulars, retain the right of private judgment; so far at least as to uphold the institution which we call the act of *Habeas Corpus.*

As for the clerical profession, several circumstances have contributed during a varied life, to diminish, so far my original respect for it, that with me the burden of proof has shifted; notwithstanding some excellent friends in it, I do not, *prima vista*, cotton to black woollen and white cravats. On the other hand, my experience of Catholic priests has operated the other way; I have found them everywhere apparently sincerely religious men, as well as gentlemen and men of the world, sometimes men of excellent education, capable of holding rational discourse without assuming a drawling voice or a saintly, overwise, eccentric, meek, or too gracious manner; I require evidence now to make me distrust them. Consequently I could look upon the ecclesiastics, of whom there are always many in the streets of Lima, without those feelings of horror with which most Calvinistically educated Americans regard them. I like the fashion of marking them by dress; it prevents both priests and laymen from contaminating each other, and organizes the force the Church brings into the field against the devil, into a regular disciplined army. Still it looks odd at first, to see the various dresses as they are seen in Lima, and in other Catholic countries. It looks odd to see an old gentleman trudging along in a light straw colored gown or cassock, with a hood for a cape, strings of beads coming round in front, a high towering mitre, a long cane in his hand, and a paper cigar in his mouth! Many of the priests wore black gowns and shovel hats, such as we used to see in the Barber of Seville. Others are in coarser robes; one attenuated old man, I remember in a gown of coarse gray, and a mitre, or high pointed cap, who stood on a landing on a broad staircase in the great monastery of San Francisco, before a glittering puppet or image surrounded by gilding and colored tinsel, (I cannot call such a gay thing a shrine,) before which lighted candles were burning; he stood fixedly for a long while with his head inclined on one side—then put out the candles and went away. It was in a place open to the public, and the scene had a pretty effect. It may be owing to early prejudice, but really the old man seemed to be laboring under a mistake; to my northern eye, he was only a fakir. At the bath house I met a fine specimen, a large round faced man, with an immense hat, and something a Falstaffian belly; we fraternized and took snuff together; he reminded me very much of Thomas Hamblin, Esq., whose death I was sorry to see a notice of last winter.

I went into the first church on the principal Calle during mass. The interior was decorated in the most gaudy style imaginable, and had an effect like that of the exhibitions of Mons. Alexander on a great scale. The body of the house was well filled with kneeling women, some of whom —one in particular, if it must be confessed—wore their mantillas, and arched their white necks in a manner that haunted my imagination for days after. I could not join in sacrifice with that abstract and devout attention, and true act of worship, which I much wished to feel and perform after my long and somewhat perilous voyage. Everything was so gay and theatrical. Still I did shut my eyes and shut out the mantilla for several minutes. The choir sung the Benedictus; the organ was out of tune, the voices bad, the music thin and common—with little of the ecclesiastical character—little to remind me of those masses of Mozart which will vibrate through my soul as long as it has life. I rose and walked slowly out. When near the entrance I turned to look back; more than half way down the church I saw the black mantilla—the straight shoulders —the proud retrorsely bended ivory neck—the dark eyes —Ah!

The monastery of San Francisco occupies seven or eight acres in the northeastern quarter of the city. It is an assemblage of ancient cloisters, chapels, and monastic halls built around and within upon many courts, quadrangles, and gardens planted with trees. On the walls and ceilings of its wide galleries and dark passages, the evidences of vast wealth and expense of labor lavished in former days upon coarse fresco and mosaic work, and curiously carved wood, are everywhere wonderful, though now all is gloomy and decayed. Here and there as we wandered through twilighted galleries, we could look into ancient cells, apparently left half exposed for effect, and through lattice work on the side walls, we saw dim lamps that are kept perpetually burning before the shrines of saints. We looked into the principal chapel; which is said to contain some original Murillos, and other fine paintings, through a side door in what corresponds to the choir in our churches, a deep gallery at the end opposite the altar. Here were two rows of monks with shaven crowns, ranged along behind a turning stand, on which were huge volumes of canticles in parchment manuscript—the letters an inch long, and antiphoned in the ancient mode. The monks were clad in coarse gowns of gray. In a stall at one side sat a middle aged priest in spectacles, who chanted while the rest answered alternately in harsh drawling voices. I could not distinguish words, and was not near enough to make out the text; the service will probably be recognized by good Catholics; I do not even know the name of it. Most of the monks cast only furtive glances at us, but the old gentleman raised his spectacles and looked at us without interrupting his reading, and some of the monks never took their eyes off us the whole time. I tried to seem much more devout than I could possibly bring myself to feel, though the whole scene, with the religious light, the vacant body of the church below, covered with ornaments and half revealed colors—all so suggestive, and realizing the imagined pictures of old romance—interested and excited me in the highest degree. I wished I could feel somewhat as the old English scholar and beautiful enthusiast, Sir Kenelm Digby, might have felt in a similar place; but my fancy is too much oppressed, too "flat and unraised;" I cannot conquer old prejudices. Perhaps it is natural to an inquiring mind, to be thought-excited by what in others chiefly engages the feelings. I was sorry that I could not renew this hurried visit to the great monastery.

The cathedral in the Plaza, in which is shown the tomb of Pizarro, was closed on the morning I had devoted to seeing the churches. Next to it is the palace of the Archbishop, forming with it another collection of ecclesiastical buildings occupying nearly a whole "block," or square

There are many others of equal extent and magnificence. None of these ancient buildings, however, exhibit anything like finish. The walls and towers are enormously thick, and seldom plane surfaced or plumb; the pinnacles upon them which are left standing rarely point straight to heaven—in this resembling I fear too many of the priests, who, like them, are said to be often sadly shaken by earthly commotions. Some of the bells in the churches are heavy, and beautifully toned. The presence of the authority of the Church is everywhere manifest. The devout bow low to the priests, and lift their hats in passing the churches, whose entrances are usually lined with beggars.

At the elevation of the Host in the morning Mass, and while the Angelus is said at evening, labor stops instantaneously all over the city, and every one remains silent and fixed, as in prayer, for a few minutes, between the tollings of the great bell of the cathedral. On a conical mountain, which rises two thousand feet from the northern bank of the river, beyond the city, stands a gigantic crucifix, visible almost everywhere in the streets. Several other peaks around the plain are distinguished in a similar manner, but none are so conspicuous. I do not know if I ever looked upon a more sublime spectacle in nature or art than this cross-crowned summit. I could never weary of gazing up to it, and losing myself in the thoughts it suggested. It seemed to shed a celestial effulgence, to radiate beams of mercy straight from the throne of Heaven.

I regretted that I could not ascend this or one of the surrounding range of mountains, and look down upon the plain, and the map of the city. But my Spanish was limited to a few words, and it was said not to be altogether safe beyond the suburbs. Besides, the weather was hot, and there was enough that was curious to occupy a stranger everywhere. I wandered off in the bye streets, and amused myself with observing the thousand indescribable peculiarities of common life. The city is all out of doors; for it never rains in Lima, and the temperature varies from 60° to 85° in winter and summer. The account in Wilkes represents it as damp and uncomfortable; but to me, in spring and early summer, it seemed dry, bracing, and healthful. One reason that everything appears so old and dingy in it, is, that wood and buildings suffer so little from the weather. Nothing grows mossy, but all is shrunken and dusty. Doors and blinds wear out purely from age, and use, and neglect. The adobe walls last as long or longer than brick in our climate. The want of dwellings for shelter is so easily supplied, that little pains is taken to make them elegant. The population is the gayest and most careless, perhaps, in any civilized city in the world; they spend their time in display, and dress, and intrigue, and live under the sky and the mountains—a joyous multitude, so happy and trifling, and full of vivacious, languishing graces, that I felt melancholy among them.

The Portales or Arcades around the grand Plaza are

filled like the fashionable promenades of any city at the usual hours for shopping and walking. They are arched porticoes, extending principally around two sides of the Plaza, and shading a wide sidewalk paved with pebbles. I read a date in the pavement 1799, inlaid with bones The shops which line the Arcades or Portales, are all open, and between the sidewalk and Plaza, along the pillars of the portico, are show-cases of small dealers in fancy goods, fringe knitters, silver wire weavers, confectioners, sellers of fruit and fresco—a kind of cool beverage made of the juices of melons and other fruits—pastry-cooks, and a variety of dealers in light goods and wares. The crowd is as well dressed as any in our cities. The gentlemen resemble the various specimens of Spanish gentlemen one often sees in Broadway. The best dressed are *well* dressed, in the best sense of those expressive words. The Lima tailors can certainly produce the most unexceptionable coats I have ever seen, and a distinctive mark of a Peruvian, high or low, is a well-shaped foot—small, and with an instep arched almost to deformity.

The ladies are much more dressed than with us; they wear no bonnets, but mantillas, which they are forever adjusting. Some of them are very beautiful, but they must wear out their beauty early; the middle-aged are either skinny or too fat—and the old, perfect hags. They have all a bolder manner than would be thought becoming except in a certain class of our fashionables. The exposure incident to more out-of-door habits tends to make them so, and their whole ideal of life must be showy and unintellectual. They estimate personal graces and exterior conventionalities more than the graces of mind and the modest naturalness of manner which we admire. I saw some beautiful young creatures with faces that reminded me of the Madonnas of Murillo, going to church, attended by duennas and slaves; the boys in the streets, by the way, were Murillos brought out of canvass into life. But it would attract attention in Broadway, I fancy, to behold a stately dame in the latter summer of youth, dressed as we should see ladies at the opera, with dark eyes and tresses interwoven with diamonds, a white mantilla or fine shawl thrown over her head, and bracelets on her arms, sailing along the sidewalk, followed by a negro slave boy, carrying her purchase of the morning—a span new silver *vase de nuit!*

Propriety, whose pardon I ask for this, without which my picture of life in Lima would be incomplete here speaks from behind her fan, and absolutely forbids the mention of many conventional differences in manners that occur there so often, one ceases to regard them as singular. "*Telle est la vie*,"—in Lima.

The *saya* and *manto*, the peculiar costume of the Limenas, or Lima ladies, is now less worn than formerly, and is, I believe, discountenanced by the most respectable class of society. Still it may always be seen in the streets, and where not fully assumed, the concealed face is very common.

The reader will have observed that I have not that cool temperament which allows one to trust himself to describe the effects of ladies' dresses, and all that sort of thing. I am obliged to speak of such matters with careful reserve. I cannot imitate our master in that department, Mr. Willis, whose vicacious sketches please the misses so well; I have too high a notion of my rank as a man; and besides, the Psyche which is confined in some bodies, is very fearful of singeing her wings, albeit already "all too ruffled." The Lima dress had always a saddening effect upon me. I felt what is expressed in Wilkes, that it is an "emblem of the wretched condition of domestic society in this far-famed city." I could not bear to see woman so degraded as to take upon herself such a character or relation to man as it implies. I pitied the poor creatures;—but we know what Pity is akin to. The very thoughts of them excite an uneasy, regretful feeling—such as a man dying of consumption, and yet retaining the zests of health, might feel in looking over a meadow in latter June. "*Et ne nos inducas in tentationem!*" was often in my thoughts. I dreaded lest I should never see my home again—should lose my pride and my soul, "this intellectual being," Mozart and Shakspeare, and everything that I care for, and subside into a mere tropical creature, studious only of ease, and contented to sport with Amaryllis and the tangles of Neæras hair. Let me be thankful that I shall have only one more regret to overcome—just an endurable little heart sickness—when I think of the black mantilla!

The saya, as it is now worn, is a black petticoat or skirt, fitting close around the waist, and swelling out gradually with innumerable plaits into long full skirts, containing many yards of material—usually fine watered silk. Formerly it was confined at the feet, and adapted somewhat to show the figure, so that the wearers were obliged to walk in short mincing steps. I believe it is worn so still, but I only saw the loose skirted saya, which swings to and fro like a ship in a heavy sea, with the wind dead aft. The fall of it from the slender waist is in graceful curves outward, and there must be as much art in the carriage of the skirt as there is in the management of a train. It has a luxurious wavy motion, as if it floated upon the air—not the sweep of the "sceptered pall" of Tragedy, but the "gilding state" of Cytherea. I could only object to the movement as being, or seeming, *too* graceful—too exaggerated evenly and sustained to be altogether natural.

Over the saya comes the manto, which is a loose skirt, also black, open down the front, and confined at the waist. This is drawn up all around backwards, and folded over the head in a peculiar manner, something like that in which our country maids throw their aprons over their heads; but so as entirely to conceal the head and face, all but the left eye, and sometimes a bit of an arm bordered with white lace and a jeweled hand, in which is often a cross of brilliants or a white kerchief. The arms are crossed upward in front, and the hands confine the manto on each side over the face. The contour of the arms and shoulders can be seen from without, the thin silk that is drawn closely over them, being their only covering. The art in which all this is arranged so as to leave only one eye exposed, is wonderful. In some instances, the fold was just held by a finger and came over the nose, giving to that little organ an indescribable prettiness. I could not help thinking, however, that these little rounded noses might, for aught we knew, be rebellious or too aspiring noses—an inch in a nose, more or less, is a great deal. But the eye—that single eye! It melts like a burning glass. I appeal to any traveller who has ever had to endure the full effect of it, if he did not feel the heat of it penetrate and suffuse him, so that it required all the ice of his cold mind to prevent being thawed, and resolved into a dew. As for myself, I could feel my heart ignite and burn out like a lucifer match every time the beam lighted on me. But then the vanity of being an object of such glances, as quickly restored and fed the cinder with new combustible material; and perhaps at this moment I am all the sounder for the repeated tempering. It is consoling to have such proof that one must be "a marvellous proper man."

It was curious to see what an intensity of expression one

little organ could convey. Some writers make the mouth the most expressive; it may be less under the control of the will. But the look can say best of all faculties, except the voice, what the creature within wishes to express. The Lima ladies have all the freedom of concealment; the disguise is impenetrable; they seem to intend to appear as much alike as possible, and it is said their nearest acquaintances cannot distinguish them. The constraint of the arms is a small sacrifice, for that, and for the display of the tantalizing voluptuousness of their figures, and the added charms of mystery. The fashion teaches and practises them in the arts of shamelessness. Without it they could never acquire, whatever their dispositions might prompt, the nerve to express in public such an abandon of sentiment.

Their style is in general languishing; but when they expose themselves, they sit straight and stately, and do immense execution with fans, as they ride along uncovered in their antideluvian carriages.

The Cholo girls, with shawls of gay colors, imitate the ladies, but with a more wicked witchery—with eyes that sparkle, and ways that make everything seem innocent. They are very free, and animated, and arch—diaboli plenæ. One morning in my wanderings I lighted my cigar where were a half dozen of them, more or less, in a room open to the street, and a fishy-eyed old fellow thrumming a guitar. I looked at his instrument—played a scale in an unusual key, and a Scottish dance that used to be in the instruction books, (very nearly the extent of my skill on the instrument;) the party fraternized at once. I was offered a chair, which I accepted, complimenting the "Senoritas mury bonitá," etc, in such elegant Castilian as one might use who never spoke or knew any Spanish, except Spanish flies a month before. I requested, as an escriba, to see the national dance, the Samacueca. At length the old man struck the irresistible melody, and one of the girls was made to dance by her mother. They brought a single little red flower, like a small dahlia with a long stem, which she stuck sidewise into her hair behind, and putting her hands behind her, and holding back her dress with her elbows brought forward, she danced and looked askance, and stamped her little feet in a way that—deserves to be brought to the notice of the Moral Reform Society, to say the least. But what I observed most was the evident pride with which the mother looked on, and the encouraging exclamations of the rest and of the old fellow, who, for aught I knew, might have been her father. They appeared to think as much of her performance as if she had played a piece upon an instrument, or sung a song, or recited a hymn. I could see that they considered her rather accomplished. This was the most like an adventure, as well as one of the most curious exhibitions that Lima afforded.

III.

"MANANA, TOROS!"

"To-MORROW, the bulls!"—was the parting exclamation of one Cholo woman to another, as I left the cars in the city on a Monday morning, the last week we lay at Callao. I remember the words; but the animation with which they were uttered cannot be pictured. Indeed, it is impossible in our cold northern climate, even to fancy the spirit and vivacity with which the Peruvians enjoy their holidays. Every Sunday is almost a festival; and on the occasion of a bull-fight, the whole City, as well as Callao, goes mad with gaiety and excitement.

On the morrow the cars were crowded, and extra trains were running between the Port and City during the day. The bull-fight began at three in the afternoon. We went up (a young gentleman from Boston whom I had known in Melbourne, and myself) just in time to be in good season for the spectacle.

The streets were thronged with people in their best and gayest attire, all wending their way to the "*Plaza firme del Acho*," or amphitheatre, where the fights are held. This is a large circular enclosure situated at the end of the Alameda, or public promenade, on the northwest bank of the river. In proceeding towards it, we followed the principal *calle* through the arch or gateway before mentioned, and over the bridge beyond it, which affords a beautiful view of the city and river, and the surrounding mountains. This bridge is itself one of the curious antiquities of Lima; it was built so long ago as 1638, and is constructed of hewn stone, heavily arched, and with massive piers in the ancient fashion. The piers being wider than the street and sidewalk, form recesses on either side, which are usually tenanted by loungers in picturesque costumes. The river lies fifty feet below, and was at this time only a series of rivulets and streams, winding about among green weed grown islands, where were children playing and groups of women washing linen. The hither or southern bank, on a level with the bridge, is overgrown with a continuous mass of the most confused and tumble down old houses imagin able—the rears of the buildings on the street running next the river. It seems as if they had been built, one room at a time, and hoisted up and left anywhere and without any regard to level, some time in the sixteenth century, when Lima was founded. The effect of the view in that direction from the bridge is, in its way, unsurpassed, and would captivate at once those artists who are fond of such subjects.

This afternoon the bridge was covered with passengers hurrying over to the Plaza. Besides the crowds on foot, were the carriages of the "upper ten;"—I wish Mr. Barnum would procure one and exhibit it in Broadway. The weight of any one of the full-sized of these patriarchal vehicles, might be safely estimated at about ten tons, more or less. But then the ladies who rode in them, uncovered, in full costume, and with fans in their hands, made one almost forget to notice the venerable arks; just as they made the dingy old street seem noble and splendid. *Their* carriage was lofty and graceful, beyond any that I ever saw, and for beauty, it may be questioned if the world can match it.

Of the ladies on the street, more than half were *tapadas*, that is, concealed by the *saya* and *manto;* and it was on this occasion more particularly than at any other time, that I suffered so much from over susceptibility. I know not how many times I lost my heart between the bridge and the Plaza del Acho. It was nearly half a mile, and as we walked slowly, there may have been fifty separate heart crackings; I recollect some of them that occurred as we met the *tapadas* in groups under the trees in the Alameda, with perfect distinctness.

The Plaza is an open amphitheatre, perhaps three hundred yards across, with two wide tiers of sloping seats around it, built within a high adobe wall. Imagine Castle Garden uncovered and enlarged, and its outer wall changed to a thick wall covered with yellow wash, and as dingy as possible; imagine the upper tier at the back within, to be private boxes, fitted up like the most decayed old wooden stable in the city—the seats below them all around only dusty stairs, and the whole coming down to an enclosed arena about ten feet below—where the bulls, and horses, and men, come in for the spectacle. Imagine in the centre a round temple, between the pillars of which the picadors can run for safety; also covered places at intervals around the arena, placed there for a similar purpose. Fancy now, for it is not my intention to dwell on what has been so often described, the multitude assembled to witness the fight; the boxes filled with beautiful and richly dressed ladies, and the seats with their motley crowd of all nations and colors, all alive with chatter, and bewitching cholo and mulatto girls in gaudy shawls. Here and there are bands of music; near us is one composed entirely of negroes, who play upon instruments like cracked hautboys. Whether their music be African, or Moorish, or Ancient Peruvian, I know not; it is almost impossible to distinguish a melody in it. I fancied it must be some remnant of the horrid barbaric noises with which in the days of the Incas, the priests hid the shrieks of the victims at their human sacrifices. Or it may have been only such as was played at the *Autos da fe*, which used to be celebrated with peculiar cruelty at the *Plaza de la Inquisicion*, now the *Plaza de la Independencia*, in Lima.

At length the President, and his family and suite, arrive and take their seats, amidst loud music and cheering. Presently several horsemen ride into the arena, beautifully mounted, and managing their steeds with remarkable ease and grace. Their horses are slender; but they are full of showy paces, and in every movement exhibit admirable training. The *picadors* assemble, dressed like circus performers, and with long red scarfs on their arms. After sufficient delay to heighten the effect, a door at the side opposite the President's box, opens, and in rushes a splendid bull, maddened by having been pricked and goaded during the last half hour outside. As soon as he finds himself in a new place, he makes a rush at the nearest object that moves—generally one of the horsemen, who allows him to come just near enough to his beautiful horse to make one's blood run cold, while the horse curvets and avoids being ripped open by the bull's horns. I shut my eyes even at this; but the fine ladies in the boxes applaud. (N. B. I should like to keep a young ladies school in Lima, and have some of them for pupils.)

This is soon over, and then the picadors, or whatever they should be called, place themselves in the bull's way, and excite him to dash at their scarfs. He chases first one and then another, and sometimes they but just escape into their safety places. Once he tears one's dress from him, and would have killed him but for the others, who come in and divert his attention. He is by this time so crazed, he sees nothing to rush at but the red scarfs, which are so long and thrown so far out, that there is less danger to the men than there seems to be. Still the boldest run frequent risks; and every time they do so and escape, there is a murmur of applause from the boxes. (Let me stand forward a little where I can scowl at this fair witch who has been distinguishing me with her glances. I will have her know what I think of her *now*.)

When this delightful sport begins to tire, out steps the *matador*, with a straight sword in his hand and a small scarf on his arm, bows to the President, and walks into the middle of the arena. The picadors assist him in drawing the attention of the infuriated beast upon himself. He holds out his scarf; the bull makes a rush at it; and just when he gives the toss with his horns, the matador lifts his elbow and drives his sword over the neck and between the shoulder blade and spine of the bull up to the hilt. If he is fortunate, it goes right through the heart, and the bull falls, almost at once, while the ladies loudly applaud; otherwise, the creature lingers a little, and sometimes has

has to be stabbed again. When he is dead, the music strikes up, the picadors and matador bow to the President, from whose box money is thrown them, horses come in and drag out the carcass, and the ladies resume their gay conversation.

After a short interval the same thing is gone over again. We staid to see five or six slaughtered in this manner, and for my own part, my heart echoed when I came away, a characteristic exclamation of an English sailor who stood near me, not very complimentary to the disposition of ladies who could take pleasure in so cruel and cowardly an amusement. But custom—and especially long established and inherited custom—still interposes a plea for them, and makes us willing to admit that in spite of these barbarous tastes, they may still not be wanting in the gentle attributes which ought to distinguish their sex. But there were some *American* ladies at the fight, looking and applauding with evident relish; and for them neither I nor any of those I was with, could feel either mercy or compassion. We all agreed, and we were some of us men whose whole lives almost, had been spent in peril, that we should have nothing to say to any American lady who could desire to witness such an amusement, after having once satisfied a natural curiosity to see what it was. That which could disgust old captains, who had seen men shot, and cut down, and stabbed, and been in affrays, and in gales and storms, and among pirates, and on savage coasts, they rightly considered they would not wish their wives and daughters to be pleased with. It was pleasant to hear many such come out with great heartiness to that effect, and show the pure gold that was hidden under a rough exterior surface, in their composition.

I am the more particular to set forth the natural feelings with which the right-minded and kind-hearted among us must regard such amusements as bull fights, because it requires no spirit of prophecy to foresee that the years are at hand when a trip to Lima, and a ramble among the scenery of the Andes, will be as fashionable here, as a tour through Switzerland and Italy is to our relatives across the water. Even as I write, the Isthmus can be crossed in less than five hours, without much inconvenience; and the recent discovery of coal beds in Chili and Bolivia, (if the newspaper paragraph can be relied on,) will soon cheapen the passage on the other side. Wherever we go, let us hope that our people shall carry with them our civilization, as they do our language. Thus much the schoolmaster.

When we left the Plaza del Acho and came into the Alameda, hundreds of *tapadas* were walking in parties under the trees, and indeed, all the way down the street and beyond the bridge under the Portales. Adopting the spirit of the hour, we amused ourselves by saluting almost every group we met, with "*Buenas noches, Senoritas bonitas,*" and whatever other impromptu Spanish we could command. The freedom was always received in good part, often occasioning much laughter among them, and in every instance the cheerful , not to say flattering response, *Buenas noches, Senor Capitan !*"—to the infinite disgust of the Peruvian dandies, who doubtless execrate in their hearts the "forineering devils" who come there and walk over their heads.

IV.

The inhabitants of Lima have always preserved their gaiety through all their reverses and revolutions. Shorn in a great measure of its ancient splendor, impoverished and decaying, as, until very lately, it has been for many years—once almost destroyed, and many times shaken and palsied by earthquakes—its streets often the scene of bloody conflicts—the "*Cuidad de los Reyes*" has continued to maintain, and has most probably deserved the reputation of being the most animated and most voluptuous city in this hemisphere, if not in the world—the city of recreation and show, and intrigue, and license. The greater portion of its inhabitants are said to provide for themselves only from day to day, often only from hour to hour, and very often will starve themselves and live in wretchedness to keep up a dashing appearance. Of course the conditions of life among such a population, and in such a climate, must be such as can hardly be comprehended among us. The wants of the people are so few, and so easily supplied, that they become careless both as to the present and future, and think only of amusement and animal enjoyment. Everything with them is unstable, unsettled, unregulated.

The political history of Peru exhibits these national characteristics in a very striking light. An abstract of the chapter upon it in the first volume of *Wilkes' Expedition*, may not be out of place.

Since 1826, when Peru passed from the authority of Spain to the dictatorship of General Bolivar, her history is only a chronological table of revolutions. As is very truly observed in the opening of the chapter referred to:

> "The history may be said to have merged in biographical memoirs of its several rulers, who have, without an exception, acted for self-aggrandizement, without even looking to the benefit of their country, its peace, or happiness."

The very next year after Bolivar became Dictator, the Peruvians effected a revolt among the Columbian troops stationed there, and elected and proclaimed President, General La Mar. In 1828, while La Mar was on an expedition against Columbia, General Lafuente, who was to have joined him with fifteen hundred men from the south, when he arrived at Callao, overthrew the government at Lima; while Gamarra, another general, arrested La Mar at the north. Gamarra became the next President, with Lafuente for Vice-President. Gamarra was the only President up to within ten years who ever served out his term of four years, though there were, during his administration, several attempts to revolutionize the country.

On the expiration of his term of office, in December, 1833, a Convention met at Lima to amend the Constitution, elected as Provisional President (the Electoral College not having yet assembled) General Don Luiz Orbejoso. In less than a month after his election, General Bermudez, instigated by Gamarra, revolutionized Lima, and dispersed the Convention at the point of the bayonet. A few days after, Lima revolutionized *him* and reinstated Orbejoso.

In February, 1835, during Orbejoso's absence at the south, General Salaverry, who was in command of the Castle of Callao, seized upon the Government and declared himself Supreme Chief. Orbejoso obtained help of Santa Cruz to depose him, Salaverry on his part obtained Gamarra. A battle was fought—Salavarry defeated and shot, and Orbejoso reinstated by the aid of Santa Cruz. Orbejoso's titles were "Citizen Don Louis Orbejoso, Great Hero and Meritorious General of Divisions, and Grand Marshal of the State of South Peru."

But the people became dissatisfied with the "Great

Hero," and the Assembly of Sicuani, consisting of delegates from four of the eight Provinces, in March, 1836, conferred upon General Santa Cruz the title of "Supreme Protector" and "Invincible Pacificator" of South Peru. He and Orbejoso entered into treaty arrangements.

At length, after conventions and doings too numerous to be mentioned, Peru and Bolivia became one government, under the name of the Peru-Bolivian Confederation, and Santa Cruz was declared Supreme Protector for life, with almost unlimited authority. The next occurrence was a war with Chili, conducted most dishonorably on both sides.

The historian in Wilkes, has a paragraph respecting the policy of Santa Cruz, which ought to be quoted. He observes that:

> "Santa Cruz's policy seems to have been to attach foreigners to his person and government, and they for the most part spoke favorably of him; but as he gained ground with them he lost it with his countrymen, and those who were and ought to have been his supporters, were disappointed and mortified to see him pursue such a course The Peruvians are conceited, proud, and destitute of that education and knowledge which would enable them to understand the necessity of asking foreigners for advice respecting their commercial regulations."

This is certainly no less true than it was in 1845.

While a Chilian expedition was preparing against Peru, Orbejoso, who had been appointed to command in the North, revolted against Santa Cruz and came to Lima; by that time the Chilian expedition had arrived at Callao. He declined the assistance of the Chilian general Bulnes, and upon the latter's disembarking his troops, marched against him. But the general who had joined him in the revolt, Nieto, kept back when he should have advanced, and Bulnes drove the Peruvians in one of the most hurried massacres that ever occurred in human history, and entered Lima. He proclaimed Gamarra President.

Santa Cruz now marched against Gamarra. Bulnez embarked his troops and sailed for the North. Santa Cruz was defeated in a bloody battle near Lima and just escaped with his life by getting on board the British sloop-of-war *Samarang*, then lying at Callao. Bulnez again returned to Callao, disembarked and took possession of Lima. Gamarra was then established, and the Peru-Bolivian Confederation broke up. Thus ended the year 1839.

In 1840, Gamarra was invited by rival chiefs to come to Bolivia and settle their disputes. But he had no sooner arrived there than they attacked him and his forces at disadvantage—routed them and killed him. Bolivia now invaded Peru—but through the meditation of Chili, a peace was brought about, "which left both Peru and Bolivia in a state of great anarchy and confusion, all men of any note endeavoring to create parties for themselves."

At the present writing there is another revolution, headed by Don Domingo Elias, who was at the head of the government in 1843 and 1844. He is a man of great wealth, and maintains on his estates a princely hospitality, for which travellers and foreign visitors have often expressed their acknowledgments. His extensive sugar plantations and vineyards lie inland from Pisco, in the valley of Ica. When I was at the Chinchas, he was the individual who contracted with the government, through their agents, the house of Barreda and Brothers, to deliver the guano. The business was chiefly transacted by his son, a very gentlemanlike young man, with a face denoting uncommon intelligence and energy of character, who visited the islands while I was there, and informed the captains, among other matters, that his father had purchased a fresh lot of Coolies to expedite the loading their vessels. The newly arrived Coolies, whom I saw, were probably some of them.

Don Elias was then said to be very popular in Peru, and his wealth was set down by common report, at six millions of dollars, chiefly in land and slaves. But it would be idle to speculate on the chances of his success in revolutionizing the country. The inhabitants of Lima will probably continue to say to one another, with almost as much indifference as we might feel in this remote metropolis—"*Quien Sabe!*"

V.

THE best account of Peru will be found in Tschudi's Travels in Peru," republished here in 1147. A new work on the antiquities of Peru, by the same learned author, is just commenced, and there is a separate one by him on its geology, which must be interesting to scientific readers.

From the first named work, I have extracted the following account of its earthquakes. Several shocks were said to have occurred while I was there, but I did not perceive them. In Callao the vibrations are so great, that all the cross-beams in houses are obliged to be secured to the upright ones by thongs of raw hide, and the whole town very often shakes like a town of jelly. The statements of many old residents with whom I conversed, confirms the accuracy of Dr. Tschudi's descriptions.

"Lima is frequently visited by earthquakes, and several times the city has been reduced to a mass of ruins. At an average, forty-five shocks may be counted on in a year. Most of them occur in the latter part of October, in November, December, January, May and June. Experience gives reason to expect the visitation of two desolating earthquakes in a century. The period between the two is from forty to sixty years. The most considerable catastrophes experienced in Lima since Europeans have visited the west coast of South America, happened in the years 1586, 1630, 1687, 1713, 1746, 1806. There is reason to fear that in the course of a few years this city may be the prey of another such visitation.

"The slighter shocks are sometimes accompanied by a noise; at other times, they are merely perceptible by the motion of the earth. The subterraneous noises are manifold. For the most part they resemble the rattling of a heavy loaded wagon, driven rapidly over arches. They usually accompany the shock, seldom precede it, and only in a few cases do they follow it; sounding like distant thunder. On one occasion, the noise appeared to me like a groan from the depth of the earth, accompanied by sounds like the crepitation of wood in partitions when an old house is consumed by fire."

* * * * * * *

"I have had no experience of the rotatory movements of earthquakes. According to the statements of all who have observed them, they are very destructive, though uncommon. In Lima I have often felt a kind of concussion, which accords with that term in the strictest sense of the word. This movement had nothing in common with what may be called an oscillation, a shock, or a twirl: it was a passing sensation, similar to that which is felt when a man seizes another unexpectedly by the shoulder, and shakes him; or like the vibration felt on board a ship when the anchor is cast, at the moment it strikes the ground. I believe it is caused by short, rapid, irregular horizontal oscillations. The irregularity of the vibrations is attended by much danger, for very slight earthquakes of that kind tear away joists from their joinings, and throw down roofs, leaving the walls standing, which, in all other kinds of commotion, usually suffer first, and most severely."

* * * * * * *

"'Atmospheric phenomena are frequent, but not infallible prognostics of an earthquake. I have known individuals in Lima, natives of the coast, who were seldom wrong in predicting an earthquake, from their observation of the atmosphere. In many places great meteors have been seen before the commotion. Before the dreadful earthquake of 1746, there were seen fiery vapors (*exhalaciones encendidas*) rising out of the earth. On the island of San Lorenzo these phenomena were particularly remarked.

"Many persons have an obscure perception—a foreboding, which is to them always indicative of an approaching earthquake. They experience a feeling of anxiety and restlessness, a pressure of the breast, as if an immense weight were laid on it. A momentary shudder pervades the whole frame, or there is a sudden trembling of the limbs. I, myself, have several times experienced this foreboding, and there can scarcely be a more painful sensation. It is felt with particular severity by those who have already had the misfortune to have been exposed to the dangers of an earthquake.

"I will here only briefly mention the celebrated earthquake of 1746, as all its details are fully described in many publications. The reader need scarcely be reminded that it happened on the 28th of October, the day of St. Simon and St. Jude. During the night between ten and eleven o'clock, the earth having begun to tremble, a loud howling was heard, and, in a few minutes, Lima became a heap of ruins. The first shock was so great, that the town was almost completely destroyed by it. Of more than 3000 houses, only twenty-one remained. Still more horrible was the destruction in the harbor of Callao. The movement of the earth had scarcely been felt there, when the sea, with frightful roaring, rushed over the shore, and submerged the whole town, with its inhabitants. Five thousand persons were instantly buried beneath the waves. The Spanish corvette San Fermin, which lay at anchor in the port, was thrown over the walls of the fortress. A cross still marks the place where the stern of the vessel fell. Three merchant vessels, heavily laden, suffered the same fate. The other ships which were at anchor, nineteen in number, were sunk. The number of lives sacrificed by this earthquake, has not been, with perfect accuracy, recorded. Humboldt in his Cosmos, mentions that during this earthquake a noise like a subterraneous thunder was heard at Truxillo, eighty-five leagues north of Callao. It was first observed a quarter of an hour after the commotion occurred at Lima, but there was no trembling of the earth. According to the old chronicle writers, the earthquake of 1630 was more disastrous."

* * * * * * *

"The causes of the frequent earthquakes on the coast of Lima, are involved in an obscurity too deep to be unveiled. That they are connected with volcanic phenomena seems probable. Lima is more than ninety leagues distant from the nearest active volcano, that of Arequipa. But the earthquakes of the Peruvian capital are uniformly independent of any state of activity in that volcano, and it is certain that the town of Arequipa, which lies at the foot of the mountain, experiences fewer earthquakes than Lima."

* * * * * * *

"On most men earthquakes make a powerful and extraordinary impression. The sudden surprise, often in sleep, the imminent danger, the impossibility of escape, the dull subterraneous noise, the yielding of the earth under the feet,—altogether make a formidable demand on the weakness of human nature.

"Humboldt in the Cosmos truly observes—'What is most wonderful for us to comprehend is the undeception which takes place with respect to the kind of innate belief which men entertain of the repose and immovability of the terrestrial strata.' And further on he says—'The earthquake appears to men as something omnipresent and unlimited. From the eruption of a crater, from a stream of lava running towards our dwellings, it appears possible to escape, but in an earthquake, whichever way a flight is directed, the fugitive believes himself on the brink of destruction!' No familiarity with the phenomenon can blunt this feeling. The inhabitant of Lima who, from childhood, has frequently witnessed these convulsions of nature, is roused from his sleep by the shock, and rushes from his apartment with the cry of '*Misericordia!*' The foreigner from the north of Europe, who knows nothing of earthquakes but by description, waits with impatience to feel the movement of the earth, and longs to hear with his own ears the subterraneous sounds which he has hitherto considered fabulous. With levity he treats the apprehension of a comming convulsion and laughs at the fears of the natives. But as soon as his wish is gratified he is terror-stricken, and is involuntarily prompted to seek safety in flight.

"In Lima, the painful impression produced by an earthquake is heightened by the universality of the exercise of the devotions (*plegarias*) on such a calamity. Immediately on the shock being felt, a signal is given from the cathedral, and the long-measured, ten-minute tollings of all the church bells summon the inhabitants to prayers."

VI.

The outrage on the American Captains at the Chinchas, alluded to in a former chapter as the "Pelican War,' occurred on the 17th of August—nearly two months before my arrival there. It was still then, however, almost the only matter thought or talked of among them, aside from circumstances immediately connected with the business of freighting. From the language of Mr. Clay at Lima, it was understood that the attention of our Department of State had been directed to it, and that the claim forwarded by him would undoubtedly lead to some satisfactory redress. But up to this date, more than eight months since the outrage was committed, nothing definite has transpired; and the circumstances of the affair are beginning to attract the attention of our merchants, and the leading commercial journals.

A sketch of the outrage, with some speculations upon it, and upon the manner in which business is conducted at the islands, may have a special interest from having been written on the spot. They are extracted from a letter which I furnished for the New York Times, and which was very kindly forwarded for me by Mr. Clay, whose opinions, I doubt not, as well as those of all fair-minded American and English residents acquainted with the particulars of the affair, coincide with those the letter expresses. The subject is important, as involving the question whether or not our shipmasters, having large commands, are entitled to peculiar protection from our government in foreign ports—a question which, in the present enormously increased prosperity of our shipping interest, is likely to be one of frequent recurrence. Probably, or at least it is to be hoped, that before this reaches the public, the outrage will have been atoned for by the offer from Peru of some proper and satisfactory indemnity.

"Before this reaches you, you will have had the news of the outrage committed by the Peruvian Commandant here upon the American Captains. The memorial of the Captains to Mr. Clay, our Minister at Lima, with his reply, will probably have been furnished in the Times. The memorial, which is a brief summary of the facts of the outrage, does not give anything like a full history of it, and conveys nothing of the deep feeling it created here, and which has not by any means subsided. The shipmasters were careful to present to the Minister only a simple detail of the circumstances of the outrage. Probably a greater or more unprovoked and brutal insult was never offered to the American flag; nor were ever American citizens so treated by an official of any foreign nation with whom their own was at peace. The statement of the memorial shows that some thirty American shipmasters (all here but two or three, who were unavoidably absent) waited on the Commandant, on board the hulk, to enquire respecting the detention of a boat's crew for an alleged infringement of the regulations, and to ascertain the views of the Commandant in similar cases. They were unarmed; they went in a peaceful, proper manner, with no other than a perfectly proper and justifiable intention, and no suspicion that they could be subjected to insult, and, least of all, to danger to life and limb. The Commandant was the agent of their charterers; he was also the Peruvian man of authority here. They wished to know what regulations he intended to enforce, in order that they might conform to them, or remonstrate, if they should deem them arbitrary, as they had a right to do, through the legal and proper channel. Nothing was further from their purpose than to oppose the measure of the Peruvian Government, or show themselves hostile to it, or offended with it. They certainly cannot be supposed to have gone on board an armed vessel *unarmed*, to insult or intimidate her commander. He was not on board. The officer of the deck, instead of sending for him, as would have been courteous, allowed them to send one of their own boats. When he came, he refused to hear them. He refused to grant a hearing to a committee from them, of one or more; but from some sudden freak of jealous obstinacy, or the mixture of cowardice and ferocity which seems to belong to the Spanish-American blood, ordered up a file of soldiers, and, before the shipmasters were aware what was to happen, had them *bayonetted off the deck* and down the gangway! It was the merest accident, I have heard repeatedly from those who were present, that some of them were not killed. As it was, several were wounded—some of them severely. It was not through misunderstanding that this was done; for the Commander could speak and understand English enough to understand, and did understand, the object of the Captains in their visit. No explanation can be given of his course, except that it was in keeping with other acts of his, though it could not have been supposed he would resort to actual violence, and only be hindered by the hesitation of his own soldiers from butchering unarmed American citizens upon his own deck. He is said to be a Mexican, who came from his native country not long ago to Peru, and brought with him all his national prejudice against Americans. He had previously shown that he meant to make all the trouble and delay he could to our shipmasters. He fancied himself in a position to treat them with military contempt, and all that sort of insulting manner which inferior Peruvian officials, who live by cheating their Government, are so fond of affecting towards foreigners. The shipmasters had felt this in the way of business; some had endeavored to conciliate him, others had been indignant by finding themselves so far at the mercy of such a petty tyrant—there was no doubt a good deal of feeling against the man, but nothing like a determination to resist his authority; and I am sure the thought of insulting or menacing him, or exposing themselves in any way to violence from him, could never have entered their minds. Such an intention would have been as far from their interests as from their duty; and to have placed themselves in such a position, with any such intention, would have been the height of madness.

I write within view of the locality where the outrage occurred; many of the shipmasters present are still here, and I have heard the views of almost all of them. I am convinced that they were most brutally treated; that they were exposed to imminent danger of their lives, and some of them severely wounded by stabs and bruises, without any reasonable provocation; and I think it due to the honor of our country, and necessary to the future safety of

American citizens, that our Government should take the matter in hand, and compel such redress as shall teach these Peruvians the necessity of caution. I hope they will be made to pay for it roundly.

It must be considered that our shipmasters do not stand upon the same footing as ordinary citizens. To them is entrusted our share in the commerce of nations. Leave them unprotected, and permit a considerable number of the most respectable of them, visiting a foreign Government ship, to be subjected to a deadly assault with the weapon of last resort—to bayoneting by a file of soldiers—and we must remodel our marine: we must have armed vessels; our clippers, now the pride of the sea, may fold their wings; we must trade with foreign nations at arm's length; and our merchantmen must be exposed to pretty much the same dangers as pirates. It is to be hoped there will be spirit enough in the present Administration to look after the affair promptly. Every American shipmaster who suffered in this assault—every one who was personally in danger in it, has a claim upon his country as a satisfaction for the peril to which he was exposed, and the wounds he received. She promises him protection; and in cases where he does not receive it, he is entitled to honorary redress.

The character of our shipmasters must also be considered, as well as their position. Here were thirty American men, each of whom was entrustod with the sole care of a large amount of property, and the sole government of a crew of men sailing under our flag. You are aware what sort of men must be selected by our merchants for such a command. In addition to the experience and skill necessary for the safe management of large and valuable ships, they must have the firmness and coolness, and knowledge of men to secure discipline on board; they must be familiar with the usages of trade all over the world, with the laws regulating their own in relation to freight, wages, crew, passengers, &c., under all the contingencies of long and hazardous voyages. There is no class of men in all the various business of the world to whom is committed so great a trust—they are so many generals in the armies of Peace. Within their sphere of business, their powers are unlimited; on the decks of their vessels they are absolute. Here are several masters of vessels whose names will be recognised in the list enclosed, whose ships and freights are each worth more than the stock of a large wholesale store, or than a large manufactory. The safety of all this, as well as its proper management, must often depend upon their lives and their discretion alone. Men are not selected for such commands whose passions or prejudices are deemed liable to mislead them; it is no part of their business to embroil themselves in difficulties with foreign authorities; they have too much at stake. They are used to look into the passions and prejudices, and bear with the suspicions of other men. I do not think that out of all our citizens, a set of men could be selected more cool-headed and fair-minded and capable of acting a manly part in any emergency, than our ship-masters; and I think their judgment and opinion in cases where themselves and their business is concerned, their views as to the propriety of what they do, and the treatment they receive, altogether likely to be correct. They are, if any can be, men of the world, used to deal with men of all countries, and knowing that it is for the dispatch of business to deal fairly, and to conform to foreign customs. They, of all men, ought to be under the especial protection of our Government. The safety of property, the security of commerce, the honor of our flag, the duty our nation owes to itself to have itself respected among the intelligent nations of the earth, require that it should see that gross wrongs to our ship-masters should be promptly redressed. It is my intention to write this with some feeling, to give you an idea of what is unanimously the opinion here respecting this affair, and because I wish to convey something more than the mere facts as stated in the memorial to Mr. Clay. By that gentleman's reply, it will be seen how it was regarded by him. I hope, for the honor of our country, and for the sake of the shipmasters here, whose hospitality I have enjoyed, that something will be done in the matter. The Peruvians have already removed their officer; let them now make amends for injuries inflicted by him when acting under their authority. It will teach them to select in future fitter agents—if they can. Affairs are by no means satisfactorily arranged here now. Kossuth is as arbitrary as such a soldier of fortune might be expected to be; he is capricious, uncertain, and unreliable to the last degree. The Commandant Serrate is probably as thorough an old scoundrel in his way as Peru can produce—which is saying something. He and Kossuth do not merely compel some vessels to lay out their full time, while others are preferred for no known reason, but they give and withhold supplying guano capriciously, apparently for no other purpose than to irritate. The whole thing is badly managed, and it is shameful that so many of our finest ships should be subjected to needless inconveniences.

"Another trouble is with the crews when lying here. Most of them have to be shipped at Callao, and are natives (Peruvians or Chilenos, called "Chols.") They are a poor diminutive race, half black, and said to be passionate and treacherous. Mixed with English and American crews, they create constant trouble, increased by the disagreeable nature of the work in loading. The consequence is frequent trouble with men. No longer ago than yesterday a serious disturbance, in which knives and pistols were used, took place on board a ship near by. Some of the men will have to be—are already, I believe, sent on board the Peruvian guardship. They will get off, it is likely, without such punishment as is necessary to secure discipline—and so in many other cases. All the difficulties arising out of this state of things can only be appreciated by sea-going persons. It has continued long enough. There ought to be an American vessel of war sent here at once. Had there been one at the time, the outrage to our shipmasters could not have occurred. An English frigate visited here soon after, under Admiral Moresby, who immediately, at the request of our captains, remonstrated strongly with the Commandant upon his conduct; and had it been inflicted upon Englishmen, serious retribution would have followed at once. It is humiliating that our merchantmen should be compelled to look for protection to the ships of England, and made to feel how true it is that English seamen are better protected than ours.

"It ought to be mentioned in this connection, that the Commandant, it has been ascertained, had applied to the captains of two French ships then here, the *Ville de Lima* and *Pomone*, anticipating a rupture with the Americans; *they both promised him their aid;* and when the American shipmasters were driven at point of bayonet and at peril of their lives, down the gangway of the hulk, the crew of the Pomone gave three cheers! This is of a piece with the doings of the French Government elsewhere in the Pacific. There is a French frigate here now, surveying all around the islands. Perhaps the next movement will be to take possession. Doubtless there is not a port in the world where there is so much American shipping that is left so unprotected as this. It is a subject of daily conversation and complaint among our shipmasters here, and any intelligent observer must confess, for the reasons above given, and many others which will readily occur to sea-faring men, that their complaints are just. The neglect of our Government can only arise from ignorance of the magnitude of the interests here embraced, both as regards the property and persons of American citizens. I understand that a memorial requesting a vessel of war to be stationed here, is about to be addressed by the shipmasters to the Department—in which case it is reasonable to hope that the evil will be remedied. Both England and America, and all other nations freighting here, will doubtless unite in urging the Peruvian Government into a more satisfactory management of the business. Whether they will effect any thing or not, however, remains to be seen; the nation is now on the eve of revolution. I believe the Peruvians need to be overawed a little for their own good, and that our ships can only obtain their freights here without unnecessary inconvenience when the authorities are fully aware that the rights of our seamen must be respected—when they actually see a force able to afford prompt protection. In such a Government as this the subordinates require to be kept in check by the presence of an authority which they shall feel it to be dangerous to trifle with. They change so often, that they care but little for the slow redress through diplomatic agents, of wrongs done to our citizens. They are fond of show, and only to be reached through direct appeals to the senses; their regard for law and order would be much increased by the sight of an American frigate anchored off these islands, and the business of freighting our ships here would go on much more expeditiously, and more in accordance with the usages of commercial nations."

Since the foregoing was written, the news has reached New York, that the frigate St. Lawrence was at Callao, and would remain there during the present unsettled state of Peru, to afford protection, in case it should be needed, to American citizens, there and at the Chinchas. This will ensure some security in the future; but if the opinions here set forth respecting the peculiar position of our shipmasters are sound, as I think they will be admitted to be, by lawyers and persons conversant with maritine affairs, there ought to be such indemnity for the past as will teach the offenders the necessity of caution.

This may be said without any personal feeling of hostility to the Peruvians. I think no traveller can visit Lima without having occasion to praise the courtesy of its gentlemen, as well as the beauty of its ladies. Although my visit was so brief that I had no opportunities to form acquaintances, I shall yet remember the impression produced upon me by the politeness of several strangers whom

I encountered at the hotels, the churches, and the principal music store. It was characterized by the refinement and genuine consideration that make one feel himself understood—as gentlemen should understand each other,—through all the disguises of languages, any where in the world. More than all its antiquities, which I wished so much to examine, and its glorious scenery, and animated streets, it made me regret that I was obliged to leave Lima so soon. I remember well the last day I was there; and how I thought to myself as the cars bore me down the plain, and I looked for the last time towards the cross-crowned mountain—" all this thou shalt see no more; and thus in a little while, thou must turn away and close thine eyes upon all that thou hast loved or thought of in all the world."

Leaving her capital with such feelings, it will not be thought the expression of a merely affected sentiment in me, to conclude my sketch by quoting and heartily echoing the sentence with which Dr. Tshudi concludes his volume of Researches :—" For Peru, Nature's bounteously favored land, let us hope there is reserved a future, happier than either the past or the present ?"

ROUND CAPE HORN.

The circumstances under which the sketches of the Chinchas and Lima were begun, on the second of December, are narrated on page 151. A few days after that, on the 5th, the Tornado took a gale almost dead aft, which lasted her more than a week, and carried her from about the latitude of Chiloe Island in the Pacific, to the east cape of the Falklands in the Atlantic. The day, or rather the hours of daylight, increased very rapidly as we flew southward at an average rate of fourteen knots per hour, and pea-jackets and sou'-westers, long unused, emerged from their hiding places. On the 5th, we passed the ship Parthenon of Boston, lying to under very short sail, so near that we could read the name on her stern. We must have presented a fine sight from her deck, as we came up and went out of sight like a gigantic phantom, in less than half an hour. The sea was very high, and she looked forlorn enough as she hove steadily up and down on the waves. I have since seen a report of her arrival at San Francisco, which stated that she experienced similar weather in these latitudes for twenty-three days!—such is the difference between going round the Cape and returning.

On the night of the 9th, between eleven and twelve, we made the islands of Diego Ramirez, which lie about thirty miles southwardly from Cape Horn, and are the southernmost land belonging to the South American continent. They are a group of high barren rocks, whose dark forms and the heavy surf which was breaking upon them, we could faintly discern in the midnight twilight, about five miles distant on the larboard beam. A thick misty scud was driving over the sky, and the strange light made the night wear an unnatural gloom; but it did not affect us after hearing the order to brace up for the northward.

After passing the Falklands we had mostly light or contrary winds till we came off the coast of Bahia. Christmas found us in Latitude 33° 24′ South, and Longitude 30° 01′ West; and New Year's day in Latitude 22° 09′ South, and Longitude 38° 08′ West. On the second of January we made the island of Trinidad, forty miles to the Eastward. This was the first land I saw which assured me that I had gone round the world—the first which I saw after sailing continually eastward that I had ever seen before. I wish to express this explicitly, for it is a fact that even among men who are capable of navigating ships, and that have often taken them to distant ports, there may not unfrequently be found those who have no clear notion of the form of the globe. It is curious to hear old captains argue upon "Great Circle Sailing," and other similar abstruse matters.

On the voyage out we passed between the islets of Trinidad and Martin Vas, and I took sketches of them, which may be useful to seafaring persons. I believe they lie about twenty miles apart. Blunt's Coast Pilot places Trinidad in Latitude 20° 31′ South, Longitude 29° 21′ West; and Martin Vas in Latitude 20° 29′ South, Longitude 28° 54′ West. Trinidad is a high volcanic isle about seven miles long and of very remarkable form. It contains some vegetation, and the Portuguese are said to have had a small settlement upon it more than a century ago; the remains of their church are said to be still visible. It has water, and there is excellent fishing around it, but the landing is dangerous in the extreme. A British government vessel was once wrecked upon it. I think my sketches may be relied upon for correctness of outline :—

Trinidad, as seen March 28th, 1853, bearing Southwest (as judged) twenty miles:—

Martin Vas Rocks, as seen the same day, bearing East by North five miles:—

Trinidad as seen January 2d, 1854, bearing East forty miles:—

Our voyage thence home was without any "thrilling" or remarkable incident. We took the Trades south of the Line, which we crossed on the ninth. In the latitude of Barbadoes the foam under the ship's head was full of astonished flying fish for several days; they did not appear to be aware that the Tornado was coming, homeward-bound. The heat was oppressive, though not so great as it had been on my voyage out, and we soon wished ourselves back into it after crossing the Gulf Stream. The moist heat of the West India latitudes is quite unlike the dry heat of the Pacific; indeed the two oceans differ greatly in every latitude I have visited. I shall never forget how we used to watch the *star-sets* in the mid Pacific, nor the cloud-views at sunsets, that I have seen "wake the better soul that slumbered" in most unthoughtful and insensible men. I am ready to maintain that the shores of the Mediterranean can show no skies to surpass those which may be seen some thousand miles westward from Juan Fernandez.

The most uncomfortable portion of the voyage home was when we were blown off by a Norwester snow-storm after passing Cape Hatteras. Not that I was particularly anxious to arrive; but that being so near, we should be so delayed. If I may make so candid a confession, the time between leaving San Lorenzo and making Sandy Hook was, in respect to perfect freedom from apprehension, and to a great extent, in personal comfort, the pleasantest I ever knew, and in all probability ever shall know in my life; for I have had so little opportunity to acquire the habits of the "parsimonious emmet," that I almost fear it is too late to think of learning them.

And here, because I wish to do it in a formal and at the same time hearty manner, let me express my respectful regard for Captain Christopher Ellery. If I were speaking at a public dinner of captains, instead of writing in a dingy composing room, and should offer that sentiment, it would be responded to with the warmest alacrity; but as a writer, I can only assure the reader that the voyage round the Horn with Captain Ellery, was more like a pleasure-trip than a voyage, and leads me almost to doubt if seamen have not exaggerated the terrors of that passage.

The outward voyage of the Plymouth Rock, (whose arrival is this day, April third, announced in our papers,) was as pleasant as could have been expected in a ship full of passengers. The only sea incident worth particularizing, was the falling in with a wreck a few days after crossing the Gulf Stream. It was just after sunset when it was first seen—a something black, that slowly came in sight and was lost again on the surface of a long heavy swell. The wind was light, and as the word went through the ship, and one after another made the object out, and some fancied they could see human beings standing upon it, the decks were thronged in a moment, the noise bringing Captain Caldwell on deck with his glass.

"Whereaway?" was his only question. He looked for an instant in the direction pointed, and suddenly dropping his glass, gave the order for changing the ship's course. The yards moved by magic. A boat was manned by a volunteer crew. Meanwhile as the ship neared the wreck, the forms upon it were more apparent. The ship was hove to, and the boat lowered away in the deepening dusk.

How still it was while she was gone! And how lonely the ocean looked! It needs such an incident, or the cry of a man overboard, when one is in a fine ship and surrounded with life, to make him realize the awful desolation of the Great Deep.

We waited more than half an hour for the boat's return. It grew dark, and another fear now arose for the boat, though lanterns were hoisted in the rigging. At length she came—a dim speck in the nightfall. She brought only the tidings that the wreck was the wreck of a brig, all under water but a part of her forward deck, and that what seemed to be human creatures, were only the knight-heads and stancheons of the rail. And so ended the incident. The yards were braced around again, and we were soon on our way to another hemisphere.

We experienced some very heavy weather in the South Pacific, and as the voyage lengthened, the tempers of many of our gold-hunters, most of whom had come from shops and farms, and had few resources for amusement, began to be sorely tried. To contribute my part to preserve them in order, I used to make catches out of sea-songs, and we got up a little glee club, whose performances were much admired. Almost every New Englander who has aught of a taste for music, has been to a "Singing School," and can read psalmody. But we had no psalm tunes for men's voices. To remedy this deficiency, I composed some for every Sunday, the last few weeks, which we sung to hymns appropriate to our situation.

Annexed are some specimens of sea-songs, which may

amuse our musical readers; the list might be extended indefinitely. What the first was manufactured out of, it is not easy to imagine. The second is a scrap of something familiar. Perhaps the third may be some Dutch melody. The last is the universal favorite. It goes to the words "Haul the bowline, the Black Star bowline, haul the bowline, the bowline HAUL!" The last word is only the cry in which all join, at the pull; the rest is sung by one alone.

I will conclude my sketches with two specimens of psalmody, by which musicians may form some idea of the capacity of our voices. They are not inserted as having any merit of novelty, but only as curiosities, from having probably been the first of their kind ever written and sung in such circumstances. The first was written for the Sunday after a severe gale, in which we had lain to for fifty-three hours about five hundred miles southward of St. Paul's Island—so that we gave it that name. The second was sung when we were within but a few degrees of the antipodes, and little more than a week's sail from the coast of New Holland. And hoping my readers feel as I do the sentiment of the words, I will here bid them farewell.

NO. 1.
NO. 2.
NO. 3.
NO. 4.

C. M.

Tempests arise when God appoints,
And mighty oceans roar;
He bids the winds and waves be still,
And straight the storm is o'er.

C. M.

Sing to the Lord, ye distant lands,
Sing loud with solemn voice;
Let every tongue exalt his praise,
And every heart rejoice.

www.ingramcontent.com/pod-product-compliance
Lightning Source LLC
LaVergne TN
LVHW010213110826
845151LV00004B/1070